INSPIRE / PLAN / DISCOVER / EXPERIENCE

TOKYO

TOKYO

CONTENTS

DISCOVER 6

EXPERIENCE 58

NEED TO KNOW 184

Left: Sake barrels at Meiji Shrine
Previous page: Tokyo Skytree rising above the city
Cover: The bustling Shibuya Crossing

DISCOVER

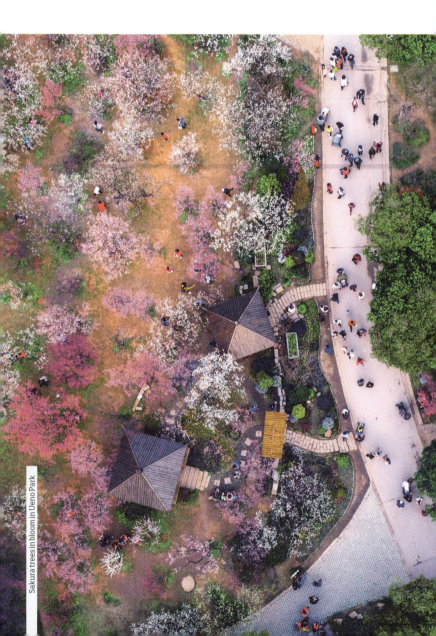

Sakura trees in bloom in Ueno Park

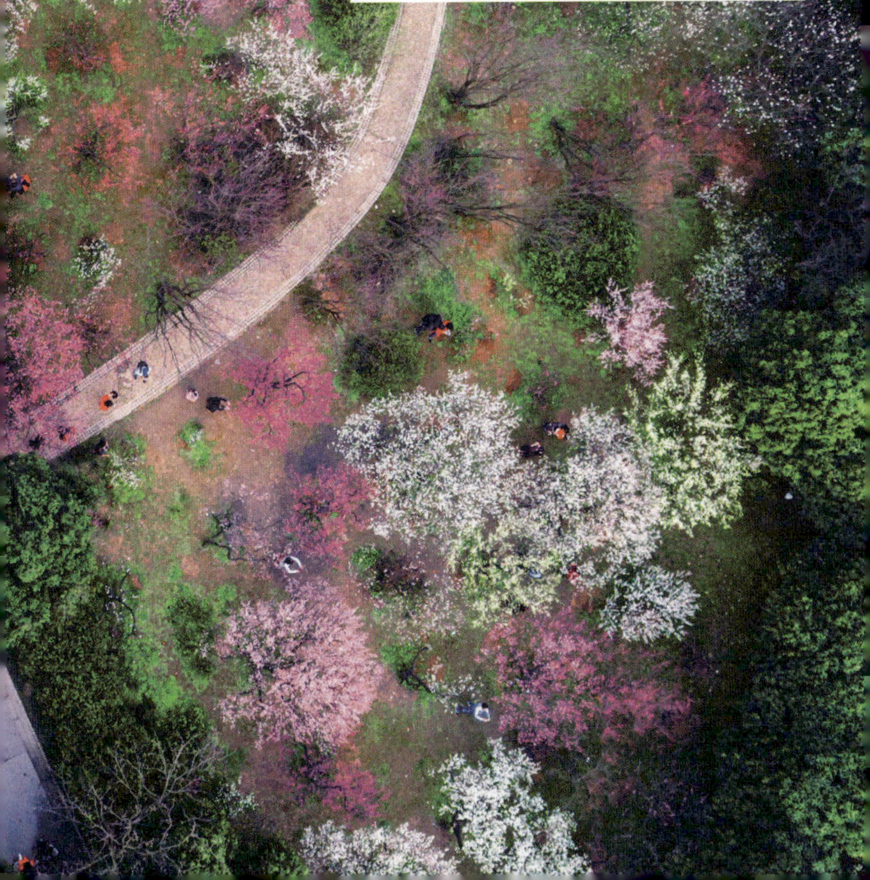

WELCOME TO
TOKYO

From the ancient and traditional to the trendy and ultra-modern, Tokyo has it all. It's a city of contrasts, where tranquil shrines and age-old festivals exist side-by-side with glittering skyscrapers and avant-garde art shows. Whatever your dream trip to Tokyo includes, this DK Eyewitness travel guide is the perfect companion.

1 Neon lights in the busy district of Shibuya.

2 Fall foliage in the Minami-Aoyama district.

3 Street-side dining in Ameya Yokocho.

4 View of Mount Fuji beyond the Tokyo skyline.

The heart of Tokyo's vast metropolis surrounds Tokyo Bay, but even in this built-up city center – the biggest urban area in the world – the districts each have their own character and atmosphere. Step into old Tokyo with a stroll through the grounds of the Imperial Palace, the home of the Emperor and his family, or head to the district of Asakusa where you'll find temples and shrines that host traditional festivals throughout the year. See Tokyo at its most chic and modern among the sleek high-rises of Aoyama, or head to Ginza for luxury shops and Michelin-starred restaurants.

But the fun doesn't stop in central Tokyo. The city's suburbs have cutting-edge scenes of their own, such as the live music clubs of Shimokitazawa, as well as cultural history in places like the sumo district of Ryogoku.

There's even more to discover farther afield, and Tokyo's excellent public transportation makes day trips easy. Whether you're seeking out ancient temples in Nikko, the cosmopolitan flair of Yokohama, or the natural beauty of Mount Fuji, you'll find all kinds of rewards waiting outside the city.

With so much on offer in this vibrant city, plus all the places worth exploring just a short train ride away, planning the perfect trip can seem overwhelming at first. We've broken the city down into easily navigable chapters, with detailed itineraries, expert local knowledge, and colorful, comprehensive maps to help you plan the perfect visit. Whatever passion has brought you here, this Eyewitness guide will ensure that you see the very best the city has to offer. Enjoy the book, and enjoy Tokyo.

REASONS TO LOVE
TOKYO

Glimmering skyscrapers, back-alley bars, serene temples, and more Michelin stars than any other city in the world: whatever you're looking for, you can find it in Tokyo. Here are some of our favorite reasons to visit.

1 THE ROPPONGI ART TRIANGLE

These three art museums in the cool Roppongi District *(p68)* carry on Tokyo's legacy as one of the world's most exciting artistic centers.

SPORTING TOKYO 2

With a fleet of world-class sporting facilities prepared for the 2020 Summer Olympics, Tokyo is the perfect city to enjoy a thrilling display of sumo, baseball, or kendo *(p50)*.

3 TIMELESS TRADITIONS

Even in ultra-modern Tokyo, the past is never far away. Shop in the old stores of the Nihonbashi district, visit the tranquil Meiji Shrine, or take in a Kabuki performance *(p28)*.

TASTE OF TOKYO 4
In a country famed for its cuisine, the capital city offers the best of the best. You'll be spoiled for choice at every meal, no matter what your budget *(p36)*.

JAPANESE GARDENS 5
Sprinkled throughout the urban sprawl are many stunning natural spaces, from secluded, meditative temple gardens to beautiful parks for an afternoon stroll *(p34)*.

CELEBRATING OTAKU 6
Geeks reign supreme in Tokyo, especially in the districts of Akihabara and Ikebukuro. Explore the arcades, themed cafés, and multi-story treasure troves of anime merch *(p42)*.

IZAKAYA EXPERIENCE 7

For a lively and authentic Tokyo night out, join the crowds at a traditionally tiny Japanese tavern, and spend the evening enjoying delicious food alongside cheap drinks.

FASHION PARADISE 8

For both chic, modern couture and quirky youth fashion, you'll find plenty of inspiration on the streets of Tokyo. Head to the Harajuku district (p72) for a little bit of everything.

9 NIGHTLIFE

Whether you're after a good whisky, a multi-floor dance club, cocktails in a sleek rooftop bar, or a hole-in-the-wall with live music, Tokyo's got you covered (p46).

DISCOVER **Reasons to Love Tokyo**

10 SIPPING SAKE

Made from large-grain rice and *koji* (yeast), sake gets its rich flavor from its unique fermentation process. Hot in winter or cold in summer, it's the perfect thirst quencher *(p44)*.

KARAOKE NIGHTS 11

Everyone from giggling teens to suit-clad businessmen belt out tunes in soundproof booths. Grab your earplugs, have your song at the ready, and enjoy the ultimate singalong,

INSPIRING ARCHITECTURE 12

Tokyo is full of exemplary spectacles of Japanese design, from the grand and ancient Senso-ji temple to the playful and contemporary Mikimoto Ginza2 store *(p32)*.

EXPLORE
TOKYO

This guide divides Tokyo into three color-coded sightseeing areas, as shown on this map. Find out more about each area on the following pages. For sights outside the city center see p134, and for areas beyond Tokyo see p154.

SUGAMO

SENGOKU

OTSUKA

KOHINATA

KASUGA

WASEDAMACHI

Koishikawa
Korakuen
Garden

HYAKUNINCHO

TOYAMA

YARAICHO

KAGURAZAKA

KITA-
SHINJUKU

WAKAMATSUCHO

FUJIMI

KABUKICHO

ICHIGAYA

SHINJUKU

TOMIHISACHO

NISHI-
SHINJUKU

Shinjuku
Station

YOTSUYA

SANEICHO

Kitanomaru
Park

ICHIBANCHO

DAIKYOCHO

KOJIMACHI

CHIYODA

Tokyo
Opera City

YOYOGI

Shinjuku Gyoen
Garden

WAKABA

SHINANOMACHI

National
Theatre

SENDAGAYA

Meiji Jingu
Outer Gardens

NAGATACHO

The Diet
Building

YOYOGI

Meiji
Shrine

WESTERN TOKYO
p60

AKASAKA

NISHI-
SHINBASHI

Yoyogi
Park

HARAJUKU

KITA-
AOYAMA

Aoyama
Cemetery

TORANOMON

UEHARA

TOMIGAYA

JINGUMAE

MINAMI-
AOYAMA

National
Art Center

AZABUDAI

Tokyo
Tower

UDAGAWACHO

Taro Okamoto
Memorial Museum

ROPPONGI

Roppongi
Hills

SHIBUYA

Shibuya
Station

NISHI-
AZABU

HIGASHI-
AZABU

Shiba
Park

DOGENZAKA

HIGASHI

HIROO

AZABU-
JUBAN

SHIBA

OHASHI

SAKURA-
GAOKACHO

MINAMI-
AZABU

AODABI

EBISU-
NICHI

SHIROKANE

EBISU

TAKANAWA

0 kilometers   1

0 miles   1

N
↑

GETTING TO KNOW
TOKYO

Built and rebuilt over the centuries after several tragic disasters, Tokyo has ended up with a patchwork of 23 wards, each with a distinct feel. The most famous sights are located in the central wards spreading around the Tokyo Bay area, but there's plenty more to see outside the center *(p134)*, and even more adventures await by train beyond the city *(p154)*.

PAGE 60

WESTERN TOKYO

Youthful and fast-paced, Western Tokyo is the place to see tomorrow's trends emerging. Roppongi's cool cocktail bars and packed clubs sit alongside cutting-edge culture in the Art Triangle, while the Shinjuku district is full of incredible skyscrapers and towers that give the city a futuristic air. But even here, Japan's stately past and traditional culture are easy to see, particularly in the magnificent Meiji Shrine, sitting in the vast Yoyogi Park by the fashion district of Harajuku.

Best for
Fashion, architecture, and nightlife

Home to
Meiji Shrine, West Shinjuku, Roppongi District, Harajuku

Experience
Joining the crush at Shibuya Crossing – or just watching the mass of people from a café in one of the surrounding towers

CENTRAL TOKYO

PAGE 86

Home to international embassies, the Nihonbashi business district, luxury shopping in Ginza, and the Imperial Palace, Central Tokyo is sleek and elegant. It's full of glimpses into Tokyo's past, in the impeccably manicured grounds of the palace and the grand buildings of Nihonbashi, where some shops have been owned by the same family for generations. This area is also one of the best parts of the city for food, with the chefs of Ginza serving up Michelin-star meals from sushi to soba. Lovers of Japanese media will also want to head here to explore the anime stores of Akihabara.

Best for
Shopping, dining, and history

Home to
Ginza, Nihonbashi, Akihabara, and the Imperial Palace

Experience
Wandering through the food halls of Ginza's palatial department stores, enjoying the free samples before heading upstairs for some window shopping (or to splash some serious cash)

NORTHERN TOKYO

PAGE 110

Sometimes overlooked by visitors, Northern Tokyo is a cultural power-house, packed with some of Japan's best museums and galleries, as well as the historic Ueno Park, the magnificent Senso-ji temple, and fascinating shops throughout the traditional districts of Asakusa and Inaricho. This area also boasts Japan's highest tower, the gleaming Tokyo Skytree, from where you can see Mount Fuji on a clear day or watch the lights of the metropolis twinkling on in the evening.

Best for
Traditional culture, beautiful outdoor spaces

Home to
Ueno Park, Tokyo National Museum, and Senso-ji

Experience
Heading up the crowded Nakamise-dori shopping street approaching the vast red lantern of Senso-ji, under the gaze of the fearsome guardian statues of Fujin and Raijin

→

PAGE 134

BEYOND THE CENTER

As the most populated metropolitan area in the world, it's no surprise that there's much more of Tokyo to see than just the central districts. In the bay area you'll find the new fish market at Toyosu and the technicolor entertainment area of Odaiba. To the north is the city's sumo stadium, in a district full of cool museums on Japanese history, as well as the vibrant Ikebukuro district full of arcades, cinemas, and the huge Animate flagship – a key stop for any anime fan. Meanwhile in the southwest, Shimokitazawa is packed with dive bars, coffee shops, and cutting-edge music.

Best for
Entertainment and exploring characterful districts

Home to
Toyosu Fish Market

Experience
Trawling the vintage shops of Shimokitazawa for the perfect outfit, then heading to a live music venue to check out local, up-and-coming artists

BEYOND TOKYO

Escaping the bustle of the city may be appealing after a while, and you can take your pick from a salty sea breeze, clear mountain air, or the sulfurous tang of hot springs. If you want to explore Japanese history, the sumptuous shrines of Nikko and Kamakura will tempt you away from Tokyo, while hikers can tackle Mount Fuji and the lake-dotted landscape around it or walk in the mountains of Hakone before soaking in its famous hot springs. Or, if you're just after some good family fun or a popular date spot, head to the vibrant portside attractions of Yokohama.

Best for
Temples and nature

Home to
Yokohama, Kamakura, Mount Fuji, the Fuji Five Lakes, and Nikko

Experience
Photographing the many faces of Mount Fuji as the lighting and weather change throughout the day

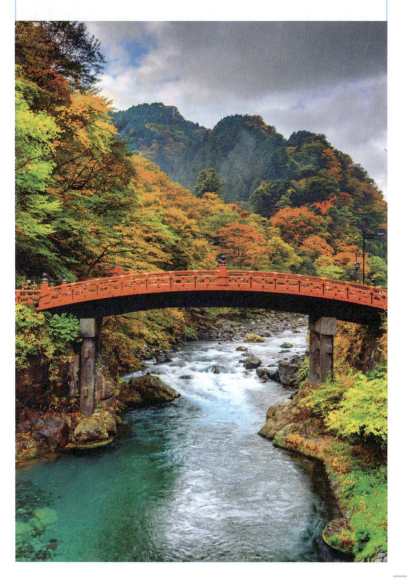

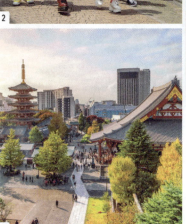

←

1 Crowds navigating the Shibuya Crossing.

2 Shopping in Harajuku.

3 Diners at a traditional restaurant in Asakusa.

4 Senso-ji temple.

An exciting mix of world-famous museums, historic temples, local gems, and cultural experiences, these itineraries will take you on a tour of the very best of Tokyo.

1 DAY

Morning

After arriving in Tokyo, head straight to the Shibuya Crossing *(p76)*. This busy scramble crossing surrounded by high-rises and vibrant ads is the site that defines Tokyo for millions of people around the world. For a unique way to see the packed crowds navigating this bustling junction, duck into the nearby Starbucks *(Q Front building, 21–6 Udagawa-cho, Shibuya)* and have breakfast at a second-floor window seat, which offer great views of the ordered chaos below. Once the morning commuter crowds have dissipated, take a stroll north through the chic streets of Shibuya to Yoyogi Park *(p80)*, where you can enjoy the wide open spaces and seasonal flowers of one of Tokyo's best parks.

Afternoon

Stop for lunch at CAFÉ Mori no Terrace *(www.meijikinenkan.gr.jp/forestterrace)*, which serves delectable treats in a beautiful wooden building made from local recycled trees. Then, for a glimpse of Tokyo's famous quirky side, dive into the Harajuku district *(p72)*, and check out the eclectic mix of clothing boutiques along Takeshita-dori. In the 1990s Harajuku became famous as a showcase for alternative youth fashion – from the vibrant colors of the Decora style to voluminous, pastel-hued Lolita dresses.

The shoppers in Harajuku wear more global brands these days, but on Sundays you may catch local fashionistas showing off their style, and the shops of Harajuku are still a great place to find unique clothes to express your own unique style. Don't leave the district without stopping off at the excellent Ota Memorial Museum of Art *(p73)*, where you can admire displays of ukyio-e woodbock prints, one of Tokyo's older, but no less popular, cultural offerings. Head downhill to Omotesando-dori boulevard, before catching the Ginza line across town to Asakusa Station.

Evening

Wander up Nakamise-dori to see the magnificent Senso-ji Buddhist temple *(p122)*. This isn't your typical, tranquil religious enclave – instead you'll find a big and busy complex full of people praying, reading fortunes, or simply admiring the beautiful architecture and towering pagoda. Leaving the complex you'll find yourself in Asakusa *(p129)*, a historic district of winding alleys and Old Town charm – the perfect place to find traditional Japanese cuisine for dinner. Nakasei *(p129)*, a tempura restaurant that has been going for almost 150 years, is a good place to sample the atmosphere that has made Asakusa a destination for foodies from all over Japan.

→

1 The Imperial Palace.

2 Tokyo Tower rising up
from Shiba Park.

3 Shinjuku's Robot Restaurant.

4 Fried octopus balls, a
Japanese street food staple.

3 DAYS

Day 1

Morning Get straight to the very heart of Tokyo with a visit to the Imperial Palace *(p98)* where you can catch a glimpse of the capital's martial past in the moats, walls, and bridges. Afterwards, duck into Tokyo Station's sprawling underground mall to pick up a late breakfast.

Afternoon Hop on the subway to Ueno Park *(p114)*. Tree-lined pathways and lotus-covered ponds offer tranquil scenes of natural beauty, but another reason to visit are the amazing museums. Make your way to the Honkan building at the Tokyo National Museum *(p118)* for an introduction to Japanese art history.

Evening Kick off the evening with a drink at the 37th-floor bar in the Mandarin Oriental *(www.mandarinoriental. com/tokyo)*. You won't have far to go for dinner because one floor up is Sushi Shin *(p107)*, a branch of the three-star Sushi Miyakawa.

Day 2

Morning Start the day at the Tokyo Tower *(p106)*, a symbol of Japan's post-war rebirth. From the observation deck, you might even catch a glimpse of Mount Fuji on a clear day. Pick up some breakfast at one of the tower's many cafés then get some fresh air with a stroll in Shiba Park.

Afternoon For lunch stop in at Tokyo Shiba Tofuya Ukai *(www.ukai.co.jp/shiba)* adjacent to Tokyo Tower, where you will be waited on by kimono-clad attendants. After a short walk to Hamamatsucho Station, jump on the Yamanote line and head to Ikebukuro *(p140)*, where you can embrace your inner *otaku* (geek) at the myriad stores selling anime merchandise, and enjoy the energetic atmosphere of the area's many arcades.

Evening While themed cafés and restaurants may have cropped up elsewhere in the world, Japan does them like no one else. The Robot Restaurant *(www.shinjuku-robot.com)* is the ultimate in quirky Tokyo entertainment, offering a loud, colorful, and kitschy robot-themed burlesque show.

Day 3

Morning You'll need an early start to get to the Toyosu Fish Market *(p136)* in time for the 5:30am tuna auctions. This custom-built facility contains special viewing platforms from which visitors can watch the bartering and bidding below.

Afternoon Take the Yurikamome line for ten minutes to the artificial island of Odaiba *(p149)*. Grab an early lunch at the Takoyaki museum *(www.odaiba-decks. com/en/takoyaki)* for the classic Japanese dish of fried octopus balls. Nearby is the Miraikan *(p149)*, the city's "Hall of the Future". Here you'll find absorbing displays of technology such as Honda's fascinating Asimo – the first robot to ever walk on two legs.

Evening Spend the evening unwinding while you soak in the warm water at Oedo Onsen Monogatari *(daiba.ooedoonsen.jp)*, the biggest hot spring resort in Tokyo. For dinner try Hamayu *(www.tokyo.grandnikko. com/restaurant/hamayu)*, where beef and seafood are grilled right in front of you on a teppan grill.

5 DAYS
in and around Tokyo

Day 1

Start your day in eastern Shinjuku *(p82)*, a buzzing district that epitomizes modern Tokyo. The area is full of restaurants and cafés, so pick whatever breakfast option catches your eye as you stroll through the busy city streets. Head for the Samurai Museum *(p80)*, where visitors can try on lacquered armor while the enthusiastic English-speaking guides give regular demonstrations of sword moves including terrifying battle cries. For lunch, grab some ramen at Tenkkaippin *(www.tenkaippin. co.jp)*; this small but lively restaurant is popular with ramen geeks who obsess over the high-fat *kotteri* (rich) broth. In the evening, head to Shinjuku's Golden Gai area *(p80)*, home to hundreds of atmospheric *izakaya* (taverns) where you can sit cheek to cheek with Japanese people unwinding after work.

Day 2

Take a morning walk through the grounds of Tokyo's oldest Shinto site, Meiji Shrine *(p64)*, which feels like an oasis of tranquility compared to the busy city

around it. Here you can buy yourself some beautiful good luck charms, known as *omamori*, which make great souvenirs. In the afternoon head to the Shimokitazawa district *(p144)* and explore this cool suburb full of independent boutiques and avant-garde theaters. It's also the perfect place to spend the evening, as the area is particularly famous for its cutting-edge, live music scene, epitomized by venues such as THREE *(www.toos.co.jp/3)*. For dinner, Food Therapy Diner Chabuzen *(food-therapy-diner-chabuzen.business. site)* is a vegan restaurant that specializes in *yakuzen* cuisine – food believed to have medicinal properties.

Day 3

In the hip Roppongi district *(p68)*, spend the morning exploring contemporary artwork at the Mori Art Museum, making sure you stop in at the open-air rooftop observation deck for breath-taking views of the sprawling Tokyo metropolis. Drop into Afuri *(www.afuri.com)* for a lunch of delicate yuzu-scented ramen and then head to 21_21 Design Sight, the brainchild

1 Shinjuku district at night.

2 21_21 Design Sight museum.

3 Sake barrels at Meiji Shrine.

4 A bamboo grove in Kamakura.

5 Lake Kawaguchi and Mount Fuji.

of fashion designer Issey Miyake and architect Tadao Ando. This museum dedicated to Japanese design is the epitome of the Roppongi art scene: cool, modern, and bursting with the artists' passion for art and design. In the evening, enjoy Roppongi's famously vibrant nightlife, choosing from the huge selection of bars, restaurants, and clubs.

Day 4

Located at the northern foot of Mount Fuji in Yamanashi Prefecture, the Fuji Five Lakes area *(p168)* has some of the best views of Japan's sacred mountain, as well as beautiful rural landscapes. Start with one of the region's absolute must-sees: a visit to the hillside Chureito Pagoda for, arguably, the best vantage point to view Mount Fuji. Have lunch at Houtou Fudou, where you can try *hoto*: the rich, thick udon dish beloved by the residents of Yamanashi. Next head to the Itchiku Kubota Museum, home to one of the finest collections of kimonos in Japan. After rediscovering a traditional technique for dying kimonos, Itchiku Kubota made it

his life's work to design and create a collection of kimonos that is unparalleled in Japan. Dine at one of the restaurants in the Lake Kawaguchi resort area, then relax on the two-hour coach trip back to the big city.

Day 5

Catch a train to Kamakura *(p160)*, a town famed for its ancient shrines and temples. For an introduction to the highlights, visit the Tsurugaoka Hachiman-gu Shrine, then admire the town's famous Great Buddha statue. For lunch, try vegan-friendly Sairam *(www.sairam-kamakura-en.link)* before taking the 40-minute journey to Enoshima *(p182)*. This little island is packed with interesting sights and enchanting views to discover as you stroll its winding paths. Aim to be at the spiraling Sea Candle tower – a lighthouse with an observation deck – to watch the sunset, and then dine at the harbor front Café Tobiccho *(www.tobiccho.com)* to sample Enoshima's specialty, *shirasu* (fresh whitebait). After that, it's just a 90-minute return journey to Tokyo.

Traditional Scenes

To understand how Japan fuses traditional art with modern design, visit Tokyo's Nezu Museum *(p74)*. Designed by award-winning architect Kengo Kuma, it showcases over 7,400 works of Japanese and East Asian art, including Irises, an exquisite screen painting by Ogata Korin (c 1701–05). Another site for traditional art in the capital is the Tokyo National Museum *(p118)*. Seek out the museum's haunting collection of Nō masks for a fleeting glimpse into one of Japan's most idiosyncratic traditional art forms.

→

Irises by Ogata Korin (c 1701-05), at Tokyo's Nezu Museum

TOKYO FOR
ART LOVERS

Japanese art enthralled Westerners when they first saw it in the 19th century, and a craze known as Japonisme swept the globe. The magnetic draw of Japanese art continues to this day, and Tokyo's galleries are the perfect place to explore one of the world's most exciting art scenes.

Modern Masters

Immerse yourself in Tokyo's vibrant contemporary art scene in the Roppongi district *(p68)*, which is bursting with galleries and museums housed in stylish modern buildings. For your first stop, pick from one of the three points of the Roppongi Art Triangle: Mori Art Museum for ground-breaking works in rotating exhibitions, the National Art Center, Tokyo, for innovative temporary shows, or the Suntory Museum of Art for objets d'art. Alongside these cultural colossi, there are many smaller art spaces, including Zen Foto Gallery *(www. zen-foto.jp)*, Complex665 *(www.tohokuandtokyo.org/ spot_177)*, and 21_21 Design Sight *(p70)*, where you can explore Japan's ultra-modern aesthetic style, and even bring a piece of it home from the gift shop.

 INSIDER TIP
Arty Stay

Palace Hotel Tokyo offers bespoke tours of Tokyo for art fans. Led by art historians, the tours take in world-class museums as well as offbeat galleries *(www.en.palace hoteltokyo.com)*.

Drainspotting

If you glance down at the street under your feet, you may find yourself standing on an unexpected piece of art. Throughout Japan, manhole covers are decorated to reflect something about the area, whether it's a traditional craft, seasonal flower, or cute local mascot. The ones near major landmarks are easy to understand – such as a sophisticated flower design by the Imperial Palace gardens, or Hello Kitty and Mickey Mouse near their respective theme parks. But you may also stumble on an interesting manhole cover down a small Tokyo side street, and learn some-thing new about the local area. If you want to become a proper drain-spotter, just bring along some paper and a pencil to create *takuhon* (rubbings) of your favorite designs – a truly unique souvenir.

→
A manhole featuring Mount Fuji and Suruga Bay in Shizuoka

↑ Emil-Antoine Bourdell's *Hercules the Archer* at the Hakone Open-Air Museum

↑ Admiring the view from Mori Tower, home of the Mori Art Museum

Striking Sculptures

You don't even have to pay for museum entry to see the most famous sculpture in the artistic Roppongi district. Right in front of the Mori Art Museum is the 30-ft- (9-m-) high *Maman* by Louise Bourgeois: a giant bronze spider with marble eggs, seeming to intrigue and terrify in equal measure. For a whole collection of sculptures – arguably the best in Japan – head out to the Hakone Open-Air Museum *(p179).* Set in the mountains near Tokyo, this vast park is full of works by everyone from Henry Moore to Joan Miro and Niki de Sant Phalle.

Ancient Sports

Developed as arts of war by the samurai, the martial arts have evolved not only into a range of competitive sports but also forms of discipline aimed at spiritual improvement. Tournaments for judo, kendo, and other martial arts are held at the Budokan (*www.nipponbudokan.or.jp*), while *yabusame* (horseback archery) is a key spectacle of the Kamakura Festival (*p52*).

A yabusame archer participating in the Kamakura Festival

TOKYO FOR
TRADITION

Though certain parts of Tokyo now look like something straight out of a sci-fi film, you can still find pockets of Edo-era culture where you can enjoy traditional Japanese experiences and customs such as the tranquil tea ceremony or a samurai-inspired sports event.

EAT

Kudan Otsuka

The perfect place for a traditional *kaiseki* (tasting menu) meal, a dining experience which perfectly demonstrates the intricacies of Japan's culinary arts. *Kaiseki* menus typically feature 10 to 12 dishes enjoyed over the course of several hours, with seasonal dishes that are exquisitely prepared and presented.

🏠 Avista Kudan Building 2F, 2-4-12 Kudan-Minami, Chiyoda 🕐 Sun 🌐 Kudan-otsuka.com

¥¥¥

Tea Ceremony

The art of the tea ceremony is a meditative and beautiful tradition, influenced heavily by Zen Buddhism. To join a ceremony, head to the historic Asakusa district (*p129*), where Nadeshiko (*www.hanayashiki.net/shops/nadeshiko/e*) offers an English-friendly tea ceremony, and the option to wear a kimono.

Classic Theater

Three major types of traditional theater are still performed regularly in Tokyo: Bunraku, Kabuki, and No. You can catch Bunraku (puppetry) at the National Theatre *(www.ntj.jac.go.jp)* and Kabuki at Kabuki-za Theatre *(p100)* – but if you only have time to catch one performance, make it No. This is the oldest and most mysterious of the three, using Shinto ritual to express a link with the gods on stage *(www.ntj.jac.go.jp/nou.html)*.

→

A Kabuki performance, using typically elaborate costumes and make-up

Aesthetics and Design

Japan's aesthetic principles embrace imperfection and simplicity, and no museum celebrates this more than the Folk Crafts Museum *(p139)*. Here you'll see many different *mingei* (folk craft) works, that prize the utilitarian aspect of everyday objects.

←

The Japan Folk Crafts Museum, founded by art critic Yanagi Soetsu

The Samurai Era

Before Tokyo was Tokyo, it was Edo: the seat of Japan's samurai government for 250 years. The Samurai Museum *(p80)* has an amazing collection of weapons and armour, and provides a great introduction to the role of the warrior class in Japanese society. You can delve even deeper into the story at the Edo-Tokyo Museum *(p148)*, where the samurai and the society they ruled are explained through life-size models, dioramas, and interactive exhibits.

←

A woman practising the elaborate ritual of the tea ceremony

→

Fearsome battle armor on display at the Samurai Museum

TEA IN JAPAN

Whatever the weather, whatever the place, tea is part of everyday life in Japan. Green tea is the most ubiquitous variety; it is served in business meetings, can be bought on the go from vending machines, and is considered the perfect way to cool down in summer or warm up in winter.

The first reference to tea drinking in Japan dates to the early 9th century, after it was brought to Japan from China by Buddhist monks. Over 1,200 years later, green tea is now a Japanese institution, and a healthy part of the traditional diet. Green tea is packed with vitamin C and antioxidants, and research has linked regular consumption to numerous health benefits – including reduced risk of cardiovascular disease and strokes, and lower levels of cholesterol.

THE WAY OF TEA

Tea was first used in Buddhist ceremonies and enjoyed at upper-class parties before a tea master. Later, Murata Shuko (1422–1502) introduced Zen-inspired ritual aspects to the custom of tea drinking. This early version of the tea ceremony was later developed by Sen no Rikyu (1522–91), the founder of the Japanese tea ceremony as it is practiced today. Known as *chanoyu* (the way of tea),

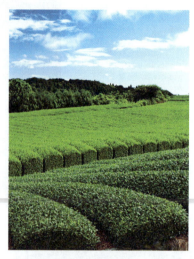

↑ A green tea plantation in the Japanese countryside

the ceremony is imbued with philosophies such as *ichi-go ichi-e* (cherishing every encounter), and aesthetic concepts such as *wabi-sabi* (beauty in imperfection). Crafts associated with *chanoyu* – including *ikebana* (flower-arrangements), ceramics, and landscape gardening – have also been profoundly shaped by these concepts.

TEA CEREMONY CUSTOMS

The tea ceremony is a well-orchestrated series of events that takes many years to master. The placement of the utensils, the moment to bring out the *chakin* (cloth), the hand to use for each movement – all are strictly prescribed. Guests kneel on the tatami mat while admiring the skill of their host, the quality of the utensils, and the features of the room. *Wagashi* (sweets) may also be served.

To drink *matcha*, bow to your host when offered a cup, take the tea with your right hand, and place it in the palm of your left. Turn the bowl clockwise about 90 degrees, raise it with both hands, and then empty the cup in three gulps.

← Pouring hot water during a tea ceremony and *(inset)* some of the utensils involved in the ceremony

TEA VARIETIES

Green tea leaves are divided into three main grades – *gyokuro*, which are the most tender, protected leaves that come out in May; *sencha*, which are tender leaves picked in May or June; and *bancha*, which are large leaves left until August.

GYOKURO The highest grade of green tea, *gyokuro* is brewed at lower temperatures than normal. It is very rich and highly savory.

SENCHA This archetypal green tea is made with whole, dried leaves. *Sencha* has a balanced bitterness, and a refreshing aroma.

HOUJICHA The leaves are roasted, producing a rich, nutty tea which is reddish-brown in color.

MATCHA A finely ground powder that is whisked with hot water. This rich, almost creamy, tea is the variety used in tea ceremonies.

MUGICHA Cold-brewed from roasted barley, toasty *mugicha* is especially popular in summer.

GENMAICHA In this blend, dried green tea leaves are mixed with popped brown rice to give a nutty flavor.

Meiji-era Surprises

After 250 years of isolation, Japan rejoined the global community in the mid-1800s, at the dawn of the Meiji era. The architecture of this period is characterized by new Western influences, with brick and stone buildings cropping up all over the city. Most visitors will come across the Meiji-era style at Tokyo Station *(p103)*, where the original red-brick building from 1914 still stands. But it's worth seeking out the city's finest Meiji work, Akasaka Palace *(p81)*, such a perfectly European-looking building it can feel like you've been transported to another city. The interior decor is an intriguing combination of ostentatious European styles and Japanese touches like samurai statues.

↑ Akasaka Palace, a Neo-Baroque residence built for the Crown Prince in 1909

TOKYO FOR
ARCHITECTURE

Wandering Tokyo's streets, you'll see a jumble of traditional wooden houses, glass-and-steel skyscrapers, and innovative tiny homes. Often combining traditional Japanese craftsmanship and aesthetics with modern materials and tastes, Tokyo's architecture is among the most influential in the world.

Traces of Edo

Many of Japan's distinct styles were developed during the Edo period (1603–1868), when the country was closed off to the rest of the world. To catch a glimpse of this bygone era, explore the grounds of the Edo-Tokyo Open Air Architectural Museum *(www. tatemonoen.jp)*, where relocated and reconstructed buildings recall the unique look of 17th-century Tokyo. The Yanaka district *(p126)* is the best place to see Edo's legacy today; its narrow streets are home to wood-fronted houses and local shrines, giving the area a traditional small-town character.

← Replica of an Edo-era storefront, Edo Tokyo Open Air Architectural Museum

↑ The Tokyo Skytree piercing the clouds high above the city's skyline

WHAT WAS METABOLISM?

Postwar reconstruction efforts in Japan's cities spawned new ideas about the future of urban planning and design. One of the most important of these was Metabolism. This movement came about during preparation for the 1960 Tokyo World Design Conference, and embraced the idea of modern cities in flux – constantly changing and adapting to meet the needs of their residents. This called for modular mega-structures that could grow and shrink according to necessity. Although frustrated in their desire to build Tokyo anew, Metabolist devotees, such as Kenzo Tange and Kisho Kurokawa, exerted a major influence on the country's architecture. Check out Kurokawa's Nakagin Capsule Tower in Ginza *(p90)*.

Modern Mountains

The Roppongi distict *(p68)* is home to one of Japan's modern marvels of engineering: the Mori Tower. This cutting-edge skyscraper mitigates the risks posed by earthquakes with 192 fluid-filled shock absorbers. These semi-active dampers are filled with a thick oil and, as the tower begins to sway – as a result of tremor or high winds – the oil sloshes in the opposite direction to balance the structure. Another modern wonder in the capital is the Tokyo Skytree *(p127)*. Completed in 2012, and designed to evoke a traditional pavilion, this tower stretches 2,080 ft (634 m) above Tokyo. This latter-day pagoda is ostensibly a TV broadcasting tower, but also has restaurants and observation decks that offer tremendous views of Tokyo.

Sacred Structures

Shrines and temples are some of the most distinctive buildings in Japan. Common features to look out for include vermilion *torii* gates, troughs for ritual washing, and *shimenawa*, the straw rope with white zigzag paper strips that marks the boundary between the everyday and spirit worlds. The Tosho-gu shrine *(p174)* in Nikko symbolizes the power of the Tokugawa shogunate. Take a two-week tour to hear an expert unpack Japanese religious architecture *(www. architecturaladventures.org)*.

←

The five-story pagoda at the entrance to Nikko's Tosho-gu Shrine

Open Spaces

Though Japanese gardens tend to be perfectly manicured works of art, sometimes what you need is just a nice spot for a picnic, or a pretty route for a jog. Luckily, the city also has plenty of parks, chief among them Yoyogi *(p80)*, a glorious mix of open areas of grass and shady stands of trees, punctuated with ponds and bridges. Beyond the city, Hananomiyako Park *(p169)* is a photographer's paradise, with vast fields of seasonal flowers sweeping towards a splendid, unbroken view of Mount Fuji.

→

A couple sit in the shade of a blossoming cherry tree in Tokyo's Yoyogi Park

TOKYO FOR
PARKS AND GARDENS

Although it's one of the most dense urban areas in the world, Tokyo has a surprising number of green spaces. Japan has a long history of landscape design, and its Zen rock gardens and perfectly manicured strolling gardens have had a profound influence on global trends in garden design.

Strolling Gardens

During the Edo period *(p54)*, Tokyo's elite created impressive gardens which you could admire from every angle, sometimes recreating smaller versions of famous landscapes, or even scenes from literature. There are still a few around today, with Rikugi-en *(p148)* being the most famous in Tokyo. Sankei-en *(www.sankeien.or.jp)* is Yokohama's best strolling garden, its small streams and winding paths creating a calm space for contemplation.

←

An early autumn stroll over a bridge in Rikugi-en garden, Tokyo

Temple Grounds

Though several temples in Tokyo have beautiful gardens, the very best are found outside the city in Nikko *(p172)* or Kamakura *(p160)*, the latter of which ranks among the best places in Japan for Zen gardens. In place of plants, flowers, and water features, these temples create contemplative areas out of rocks and moss.

→

The teahouse and rock garden in the Jomyo-ji temple grounds in Kamakura

Modern Outdoors

Parks and gardens are still an obsession in Tokyo, and inhabitants of this ever more crowded city continue to find ways to bring nature into their daily lives. One great example is in the luxurious Ginza Six building *(p90)*, where you'll find a sleek rooftop garden with views of the Ginza district. Inside, the garden is continued with two "living walls" – one covered in real plants, the other showing a digital waterfall.

→

Getting some fresh air on the roof of Ginza Six

A serving of soba noodles with a side of tempura, a staple at Japanese tables

Oodles of Noodles

In Tokyo you're never far away from a steaming bowl of this much-loved national staple. There are three main forms of noodles here: Chinese-style ramen wheat noodles, light soba (buckwheat noodles), and unctuous udon (white wheat noodles). Each region in Japan has their own twist, but you can sample them all at the Shin-Yokohama Raumen Museum in Yokohama *(www. raumen.co.jp)*.

TOKYO FOR
FOODIES

Tokyo's fascinating food culture encompasses everything from the cheap charms of *combini* (convenience stores) to more Michelin stars than any other city on the planet. There's too much to sample in one trip, but here are a few of the best ways to make the most of every meal in Tokyo.

EAT

In the basement of Tokyo's department stores you'll often find a huge food hall, where you can pick up lunch, snacks, and free samples.

Shinjuku Takashimaya
📍5-24-2 Sendagaya, Shibuya ⓦtakashi maya-global.com

Ikebukuro Tobu
📍1-1-25 Nishi-Ikebukuro, Toshima ⓦtobu-dept. jp/ikebukuro

Nihombashi Mitsukoshi
📍1-4-1 Nihombashi, Chuo ⓦmitsukoshi. mistore.jp/nihombashi. html

Let's Roll!

There are hundreds of different flavors and types of sushi, but in its purest form, this delicacy is about two things: rice and fish. Chefs train for a lifetime before they can claim to master this deceptively simple dish, but don't let this put you off trying your hand at rolling your own: the world-famous Toyosu Fish Market *(p136)* is a fitting place to learn with Sushi Mafia *(www.sushi.tokyo.jp)*.

Sweet Treats

Tokyo is a great city for traditional Japanese dishes, including dessert. In big train stations and department stores you'll see beautifully presented boxes of *wagashi* – Japanese confectionery flavored with fruit or beans. More casual snacks to try include *taiyaki* (fish-shaped pastries) and *kakigori* (syrup over shaved ice). You'll also find many Western desserts with a Japanese twist: crepes are the stars in Shibuya, while parfait is synonymous with Tokyo's upmarket cafés.

→

Beautiful and delicate *wagashi* sweets made for the summer season

Michelin-starred

With a total of 230 Michelin stars in Tokyo, fans of fine dining are spoiled for choice. For a quintessentially Japanese option, Daigo *(www.atago-daigo.jp)* is a sublime introduction to *shojin ryori*, the vegetarian cuisine developed in accordance with Buddhist principles.

←

Chef Kenji Nagata of Azabu Yukimura, a traditional Japanese restaurant with three Michelin stars

Local Markets

For a bite on the go, nothing beats a trip to a food market. One of the city's most beloved and long-standing is Ameya Yokocho *(p126)*, frequented as much by locals buying groceries as tourists looking for snacks and souvenirs. At seasonal *matsuri* (festivals) you can expect street food stalls to appear, too.

←

Showcasing the endless variety of sushi types, from nigiri to makidaywork

→

Fresh seafood on sale at Ameya Yokocho market in Ueno

Cheap Eats

Vending machine restaurants offer affordable and filling food, and a slice of real Tokyo life. Insert some yen into the slot, select a meal, and a ticket will pop out. Give this to the cook at the counter in return for a steaming bowl of ramen or a piled plate of fluffy rice. Yoshinoya, the oldest fast-food restaurant in Tokyo, has served up *gyudon* – a hearty dish of rice, beef, and onion – since 1899 *(www.yoshinoya.com)*. If you're on the go, *combinis* (convenience stores) are a great place to pick up some cheap and tasty food, especially *onigiri* (rice balls).

→

Eating *gyudon* at a communal table at Tokyo's Yoshinoya

TOKYO
ON A SHOESTRING

Tokyo has a reputation for being expensive, but there are plenty of ways to save your yen, from eating classic convenience store fare to using special discount passes for museum entry. With a bit of planning and imagination, Tokyo is a very budget-friendly destination.

Entertainment for Less

If you're interested in seeing Kabuki but don't want to spend a lot of money on a play you can't really follow, *hitomaku-mi* – or single-act – tickets are the perfect choice. They enable you to watch just one act of a play at Tokyo's Kabuki-za *(p101)*, which could last anything from 15 minutes to an hour, with prices on a sliding scale. If you'd rather be the performer than the audience, make a beeline for one of the city's karaoke spots for a night of cheap but highly entertaining and ultra-Japanese fun. Karaoke Kan and Karaoke no Tetsujin are cheap and popular chains, while Karaoke Uta Hiroba includes soft drinks in the price. Look out for *nomihoudai* (all-you-can-drink) promotions if you need some Dutch courage before your first song.

 INSIDER TIP
Discount Passes

Grutto Pass offers discounts for museums in Tokyo *(www.rekibun. or.jp)*, while Odakyu has lots of options for attractions farther afield *(www.odakyu.jp)*.

STAY

9h nine hours

Staying at a capsule hotel is a great way to combine affordable and quality overnight accommodation with a true Tokyo experience. 9h nine hours has several locations in Tokyo - one exclusively for women - where you can enjoy the simple and efficient capsule hotel system.

🏠 3-11-15 Kanda Nishikicho, Chiyoda
🌐 ninehours.co.jp

Ⓨ Ⓨ Ⓨ

→ The 9h nine hours Takebashi capsule hotel in central Tokyo

↑ Actors Onoe Kikugoro and Nakamura Baigyoku performing Kabuki

Cultural Spots

Among Tokyo's profusion of historic buildings and impressive museums, you'll also find spots to soak up some culture free of charge. For something traditional, the Imperial Palace *(p98)* offers complimentary tours of the grounds most days. And for lovers of Japanese pop culture, the Tokyo Anime Center *(www.animecenter.jp)* hosts free exhibits throughout the year.

↑ The grounds of the Imperial Palace can be visited during free tours

Games Galore

For some raucous fun that's also a quintessential Tokyo experience, explore one of the city's many arcades. Video games, prize machines, photo booths – these entertainment centers will provide hours of fun for kids of any age. For the best of the best, nothing beats SEGA Joypolis in Odaiba *(www.tokyo-joypolis.com)*, a cross between an arcade and a theme park which has everything from the typical rhythm games and crane machines to anime-themed attractions and virtual reality rollercoasters. Make a day of it in Odaiba *(p148)* by visiting the giant Gundam robot statue and enjoying the view from the Giant Sky Wheel ferris wheel.

→

Odaiba's Giant Sky Wheel and *(inset)* the popular *Taiko no tatsujin* drum rhythm game

TOKYO FOR
FAMILIES

While Tokyo seems more like an adult's playground, kids have lots to get excited about, including fascinating museums, vibrant theme parks, and fun festivals. For a breath of fresh air, head out of the metropolis to try outdoor activities in the lakes and mountains of inland Japan.

Museums They'll Love

Among Tokyo's many and varied museums, there are plenty which encourage kids to get involved with hands-on exhibits. At the Edo-Tokyo Museum in Ryogoku *(p148)* you can wander through reconstructed streets from Tokyo's past, while the Miraikan *(p149)* takes you into the city's future with robot demonstrations and a focus on science and technology. For some cartoon magic come to life, the Ghibli Museum *(p141)* immerses visitors in the worlds of classic anime films including *My Neighbor Totoro* and *Castle in the Sky*.

←

Children playing on the "Cat Bus" at the charming Ghibli Museum

TOP 3 PARKS TO TAKE A BREAK

Inokashira Park
Go boating on the lake then visit the nearby Ghibli Museum (p141).

Ueno Park
Wide green spaces perfect for picnics and letting off steam (p114).

Yoyogi Park
After joining the crowds at Harajuku and Meiji Shrine, take a break in this wooded park in Shibuya. (p80)

Culture for Kids

Japanese summer *matsuri* (festivals) tend to be bright, high-energy events, with traditional customs such as dances and parades in addition to street food and fireworks displays. Dress in *yukata* (cotton kimono) for the full *matsuri* experience. Whatever time of year you visit, a soak in an *onsen* (hot springs) is a delight after a long day. In Tokyo, Oedo Onsen Monogatari (daiba.ooedoonsen.jp) makes a good introduction, but there are more authentic options in Hakone (p178).

→

Glowing paper lanterns at a summer festival at Yasukuni Shrine

Grand Days Out

While there are other Disney resorts in the world, the one in Tokyo (p181) is a real must see, with rides, parades, and characters exclusive to Japan. If you'd rather avoid the entry fees, head to Yokohama for the day instead. The relaxed, international feel of this city makes an interesting contrast to Tokyo, and kids will love riding the ferris wheel and trying panda-shaped steamed buns in Chinatown. The Fuji Five Lakes (p168) are another great option, with enchanting spots to explore like the Kawaguchiko Music Forest, and lots of opportunities for outdoor adventures.

←

Posing in front of the iconic Cinderella Castle in Tokyo Disneyland

Theme Cafés Galore

Giant merchandise retailer Animate runs several theme cafés across Tokyo *(cafe. animate.co.jp)*. The venues change their theme regularly, each one dedicated to a different anime and serving up themed menus and exclusive merchandise. Arrive early to reserve a dining slot for the day, and if you can't get in (they get booked up fast) you can console yourself at one of the permanent anime or cartoon themed cafés that dot the city, with places based on Square Enix series, Pokémon, Gundam, Peanuts, and more.

→

Pikachu-themed treats at the Nihonbashi Pokémon Café

TOKYO FOR
GEEKS

From black-and-white manga to high-tech video games, Japan's geeky cultural exports have won legions of followers around the world. For these passionate fans, Tokyo is nothing less than paradise: a city where whole districts have become playgrounds for *otaku* (geeks) of all kinds.

Serious Shopping

A lot of Tokyo's geek action takes place in three areas of the city. The Akihabara district *(p96)* is the official face of the community, and it's here that ubiquitous *otaku* icons like maid cafés and J-Pop idol band AKB48 were born. While Akihabara is geared more toward men, female fans will feel at home in Ikebukuro *(p140)*, where many stores focus on the genres and series most popular with women. Finally, the Nakano Broadway mall *(www.nbw.jp)* is where Mandarake's second-hand-goods empire is located. With dozens of shops, each devoted to a different genre, it's the perfect place to hunt down rare merch.

 PICTURE PERFECT
Anime Tourism

Seichi junrei is the term for anime sightseeing: visiting real-life places used in anime. The hobby is often paired with *butaitanbou,* the act of taking photos of the locations to closely match the anime scene.

Best. Conventions. Ever.

The *otaku* calendar is full of exciting events all year round, and most of the bigger ones are held in and around Tokyo – including AnimeJapan (*www.anime-japan.jp*), where the anime industry shows off its latest products. There's also the mammoth Comiket convention (*www.comiket.co.jp*), held twice a year at Tokyo Big Sight (p149).

Inaugurated in 1971, not only is Comiket the world's biggest *dojinshi* (fan comics) fair, it's also Japan's largest *otaku* gathering, attracting around half a million people.

← Cosplayers posing for a photo at a fan convention

ANIME PHOTO OPS

Seiseki-Sakuragaoka
📍 1-10-10 Sekido, Tama-shi
The setting of Studio Ghibli's *Whisper of the Heart*. A map at the station helps you find the film's locations.

Asakusa and Kappabashi-dori
Fans of the hit 2019 anime *Sarazanmai* can wander around these areas to find familiar locations around every corner (p128).

Suga Shrine Stairs
📍 5 Sugacho, Shinjuku
Visit these stairs for a photo replicating the finale of the second highest-grossing Japanese film of all time: *Your Name.*

↑ Hello Kitty and a guest participating in a hug-a-thon event held at Sanrio Puroland

↑ Colorful shops signs in Akihabara, Tokyo's main geek district

</Reality>

If you're not satisfied with simply shopping, dining, and cosplaying, immerse yourself even more in your favorite fantasy worlds at one of Tokyo's theme parks. Lovers of all things ultra-cute can visit Sanrio Puroland (p181) to meet the adorable Hello Kitty and friends. For something more mature, *Neon Genesis Evangelion* fans can travel to Fuji Q Highland (p181) for a chance to explore the Nerv HQ and admire a model of Eva Unit 01.

Get a Grape

Japan's wine industry is growing rapidly in both size and international acclaim – all the more reason to visit Tokyo's neighbor, Yamanashi Prefecture, where around 30 per cent of Japanese wine is produced. To sample lots of local labels, Budo no Oka *(p181)* offers tastings of over 150 varieties from their cellar, amid Yamanashi's beautiful rural scenery.

→

Grapes growing at a vineyard in Katsunuma, Yamanashi Prefecture

TOKYO
RAISE A GLASS

Japan has made its mark on drinks of all varieties, from original beverages like sake to international imports like whisky. You can enjoy all of them to the full in the Tokyo area, the city with arguably the most diverse drinking scene in the world and a paradise for connoisseurs of fine alcohol.

For Goodness' Sake

Sake is Japan's traditional alcohol, and any trip to Tokyo should include a tasting session. A good place to start is Kuri *(www7a.biglobe. ne.jp/~kurisake)*, a standing bar chain with an excellent sake selection. Otherwise go on a shopping spree at Kimijimaya Ginza *(1-Chome-2-1, Ginza, Chuo)*, which stocks 300 types of sake and has its own tasting bar.

Traditional sake serving, pouring from a *tokkuri* flask into an *o-choko* cup ↑

Neat Drinks

When commercial whisky production began in Japan in 1924, nobody would have guessed that the nation would rise to the top of whisky world. Today the likes of Suntory and Nikka are on equal footing with the best Scottish and Irish labels, and frequently win awards at prestigious competitions. The best way to experience Japan's amazing whisky is visiting the Suntory Hakushu Distillery *(p181)* in Yamanashi Prefecture. Here you can choose a free tour of the museum and facilities, or a guided tour (for a fee) where you can watch the production process and taste their world-famous Hakushu Single Malt Whisky.

Seiichi Koshimizu, a chief blender at one of Suntory's distilleries

TOP 3 GLAMOROUS BARS

The Peak Bar
🏨 Park Hyatt Tokyo 41F, 3-7-1 Nishi-Shinjuku, Shinjuku
Admire Shinjuku's skyscrapers from this high perch in the Park Hyatt Hotel.

TwentyEight
🏨 Conrad Tokyo 28F, 1-9-1 Higashi-Shinbashi, Minato
The bar's huge windows offer unbeatable views over the Hama-rikyu Gardens, the Rainbow Bridge, and Tokyo Bay.

The Lobby Lounge and Bar
🏨 Tokyo Midtown 45F 9-7-1 Akasaka, Minato
This stylish bar on the 45th floor of the Ritz-Carlton Hotel has a chic fusion of Japanese and Western decor.

Craft Beer Scene

Tokyo's craft beer scene is enjoying a significant boom, with lots of enterprising brewers not afraid of experimenting with flavors and ingredients. Start with a trip to Popeye *(2 Chome-18-7 Ryogoku, Sumida)*: with 70 beers on tap, this specialist haunt has by far the largest range of Japanese beers in the world. Then visit Nakameguro Taproom *(www. bairdbeer.com/taprooms/nakameguro)* whose lineup is totally comprised of fine drinks by Baird Brewing, one of the best craft breweries in Japan.

↑ A bartender serving craft beer at Popeye in Ryogoku

Izakaya

Izakaya are down-to-earth taverns where you eat as you drink (rather than vice versa), ordering a few dishes at a time. Places like Shirube Shimokitazawa *(2 Chome-18-18-2 Kitazawa)* stay largely traditional but with a modern twist, while others like Gonpachi *(www.gonpachi.jp/nishi-azabu)* add live performances to the *izakaya* formula.

→

Customers enjoying a drink under the red lanterns of an *izakaya*

TOKYO
AFTER DARK

Tokyo comes alive at night, when workers pour out of their offices and into *izakaya* (Japanese taverns), up-and-coming DJs and musicians fill the dancefloors and live houses, and visitors enjoy the city lights over a glass of world-class whisky.

TOP 3 **NIGHTLIFE DISTRICTS**

Shibuya
Young, cool, and vibrant, Shibuya nightlife is a microcosm of the city. Whether you want a jazz café, a nightclub, or karaoke, you'll find it here *(p84)*.

Roppongi
This district is famed for its hedonistic club scene, and is particularly popular with expats *(p68)*.

Shimokitazawa
Come here for vinyl-only DJ sets, live music, and laidback bars. This relaxed district is the place to go to find the trends of tomorrow *(p144)*.

A performer at Tokyo's high-energy Robot Restaurant ↑

LGBT+ Tokyo

Tokyo has undoubtedly the most active LGBT+ scene in Japan, and most of it is centered in an area of Shinjuku known as "Ni-Chome". As well as the highest concentration of gay bars in the world, you'll find community culture in places like Okamalt, an LGBT+ book café (2-Chome-18-10). Spring is a great time to visit, as many venues have special events or promotions to celebrate Tokyo Rainbow Pride.

$\rightarrow$

Participants enjoying a Tokyo Rainbow Pride event

Join the Club

When Tokyoites go clubbing they make a night of it – the last train home is so early that you may as well dance until 5am. Though the city is particularly famous for its shoebox-sized venues, there are a few exceptions, including mega-club ageHA (www. ageha.com), and the Shibuya district's ever-popular Womb (www.womb.co.jp).

$\leftarrow$

Taking a break from the dance floor at the bar of WWW, a Shibuya nightclub

Quirky Nights

Even if you're not keen on the club scene, it's worth venturing out into Tokyo after dark to try one of the city's many unique evening experiences. Where else in the world can you enjoy dinner and a robot show, as at the Robot Restaurant (www.shinjuku-robot.com/sp)? Or order cocktails with a side of spiritual advice at Vowz (www. vowz-bar.com), the cozy Shinjuku bar run by Buddhist monks?

$\uparrow$ The popular girl group AKB48 have a theater and café in Akihabara

Tokyo Live!

Tokyo is teeming with places to hear live music of all kinds. Head to Shimokitazawa (p144) to hear local emerging artists, while fans of mainstream J-Pop should check out the AKB48 Theater in Akihabara (p96).

Secret Shrines

There are thousands of shrines and temples in Tokyo, and most look so similar that after a while they become a blur. Until, that is, you find something unique like Kanda Myojin *(p108)*. Although it's one of Tokyo's oldest shrines, its proximity to the Akihabara electronics district has made Kanda Myojin a surprisingly modern place. It now offers blessing ceremonies for computers and *omamori* (good luck charms) to protect your tech from viruses. Other underrated shrines in Tokyo include the Nezu Shrine *(1 Chome-28-9 Nezu, Bunkyo)* which has an awe-inspiring *torii* tunnel the likes of which you'd find in Kyoto. There's also a photogenic figurine collection at Gotokuji *(2-Chome-24-7 Gotokuji, Setagaya)* which is said to be the origin of the *maneki-neko* (lucky beckoning cat statue).

$\rightarrow$

Walking through the tunnel of vermillion torii gates at Nezu Shrine

TOKYO
OFF THE BEATEN PATH

Tokyo is full of surprises and rewards for curious travelers who are not afraid of venturing off the beaten track. A trip to see Tokyo's hidden gems is an excellent way to get to know the city in a different, more intimate way when you're done visiting its famous highlights.

Old Neighborhoods

If you ever feel like escaping the busy, neon-lit hubbub of central Tokyo, find refuge in one of the city's remaining Shitamachi (lower city) districts which provide a taste of Old Town Tokyo. These neighborhoods are characterized by narrow winding streets full of flower pots, dozing cats, and small independent shops and cafés. Yanaka *(p126)* still has that genuine Shitamachi feel, and makes the perfect place for a peaceful stroll or lunch away from the city crowds.

$\leftarrow$

A shopfront in Yanaka, decorated with the *maneki-neko* (beckoning cat)

TOP 3 **TOKYO SENTO (PUBLIC BATHS)**

Takara-yu
🏠 27-1 Senju Motomachi, Adachi
This *sento* has a lovely garden and koi pond.

Shimizu-yu
🏠 3 Chome-9-1 Koyama, Shinagawa
The only *sento* in Tokyo with two different kinds of hot spring water – black and gold.

Myojin-yu
🏠 5 Chome-14-7 Minamiyukigaya, Ota
Built in the temple style typical of Tokyo *sento*.

Quirky Museums

With its colorful fashion districts, wacky theme cafés, and noisy arcades, Tokyo is a haven for the weird and wonderful. While touring the city, you may even stumble across whole museums dedicated to strange and delightful topics, such as the tiny Kite Museum *(1 Chome-12-10 Nihonbashi, Chuo)*. Even neighboring Yokohama gets in on the action, with its Cup Noodles Museum *(p158)* being an unexpectedly vast, detailed, and stylish museum.

Instant Noodle History Cube exhibit at the Cup Noodles Museum ↑

Back to Nature

The Prefectures around Tokyo are full of refreshing rural spaces *(p150)*, but you don't have to go too far to find unspoiled nature. Todoroki Valley has an attractive, riverside walking trail that can be completed in around 30 minutes. The gorge itself is beautiful and relaxing, and along the riverbanks you'll find Shinto shrines, Buddhist temples, and a small tearoom.

→

A log bridge over the Yazawa River in Todoroki Valley

Try Hard

Japan's love affair with rugby started in the mid-19th century with the end of isolationism, and it was soon a regular fixture at elite universities. It became a true favorite and a source of national pride after Japan's team – the Brave Blossoms – put together a string of impressive performances and a legendary last-minute victory over South Africa in 2015. Although the World Cup may be over, rugby fever is still running high, so it's well worth booking tickets to a match to join in Tokyo's newfound sporting obsession *(www.rugby-japan.jp)*.

→

Japan playing against South Africa in the 2015 Rugby World Cup

TOKYO FOR
SPORTS FANS

With the Rugby World Cup and Summer Olympics and Paralympics getting everyone in the city fired up, there's no better time to be a sports fan in Tokyo. Experience the energy and excitement for yourself by mingling with locals at a baseball game or a sumo match, or just hanging out in a good sports bar.

Competitors fighting kendo-style with bamboo swords ↓

Martial Arts

From the dramatic silence of *kyudo* archers to the war-like shouts of *kendo* swordsmen, the martial arts provide all kinds of thrilling spectacles. Tournaments are often held at Tokyo Budokan *(www.nipponbudokan.or.jp)*, with demonstrations held in February. Other events occur in April at the Taito Riverside Sports Center *(1 Chome-1-10 Imado, Taito)*, and November at Meiji Shrine *(p64)*.

Hit a Home Run

Baseball was imported to Japan from the US during the early Meiji Period *(p55)*, and almost immediately gained popularity among amateur athletic clubs and universities. Banned as a corrupting American influence during World War II, it is now the most watched and played sport in the country. The season runs from late March to early October, and tickets are easy to buy on each team's website. Tokyo's own Yomiuri Giants *(www.giants.jp/en/ticket)* probably offer the most lively experience, as they have both the most avid fans and die-hard haters, known as the *anchi-Jaiantsu* (anti-Giants).

← Yomiuri Giants fans enjoying a baseball game at their home stadium, the Tokyo Dome

DRINK

MLB café Tokyo
This shrine to baseball is packed with memorabilia of Japan's favorite sport.

🅰 1-3-61 Kouraku
🅦 mlbcafe.jp

Los Cabos Shinjuku
A Mexican-style sports bar with great tequila.

🅰 1-3-16 Kabukicho
🅦 pasela.co.jp/shoplist/loscabos/shinjuku

Legends Sports Bar
Enjoy juicy burgers and craft beer as you watch different sports on the bar's eight screens.

🅰 3-16-33 Roppongi
🅦 legendsports.jp

RINGS OF GLORY

The 1964 Summer Olympics and Paralympics in Tokyo symbolized Japan's rebirth after World War II. Many Japanese people see the 32nd Olympiad in 2020 as a similarly significant and renewing event, marking the end of the difficult few decades since the economic bubble burst in the early 1990s. Despite controversies and a major redesign, the huge New National Stadium promises to be a monument to match those from the last Olympics. Hire a bike, and cycle around Yoyogi Park *(p80)* to admire some of the original 1964 venues that will be used once again in 2020.

Sumo wrestlers and a *gyoji* (referee) ↑

Want Sumo This?

Sumo matches are an incredible display of pomp and power, with pre-bout posturing before wrestlers collide into each other with a crash that sends gasps around the arena. Tokyo's spectacular Ryogoku Kokugikan venue hosts three grand tournaments a year, and tickets go on sale a month in advance *(www.sumo.or.jp/EnTicket)*. Between events, the *beya* – where the wrestlers live and train – open their doors to visitors. To catch an early morning training session, contact the Japan Sumo Association *(sumo.or.jp)*.

A YEAR IN
TOKYO

JANUARY

New Year (*Jan 1*). At midnight, the bells of Senso-ji temple toll a total of 108 times.

△ **Sumo** (*late Jan*). At Ryogoku Kokugikan, a major sumo tournament (called honbasho) is held to celebrate the new year.

FEBRUARY

△ **Setsubun** (*Feb 3*). To celebrate the start of spring, beans are thrown to scare away evil and bring good fortune.

Valentine's Day (*Feb 14*). Lavish chocolates and romantic gifts are sold in stores, though in Japan it is only women who give gifts on Valentine's Day.

MAY

Childrens Day (*May 5*). To celebrate Children's Day, 333 carp-shaped streamers (one for each meter of the tower), are displayed at Tokyo Tower.

△ **Sanja Matsuri** (*3rd weekend in May*). Around one hundred portable shrines (*mikoshi*) are carried through the streets of Asakusa to bring good fortune to the local businesses and residents.

JUNE

△ **Ajisai Viewing** (*mid-Jun*). Meigetsu-in temple in Kamakura has a particularly spectacular display of June's seasonal flower: hydrangeas.

Fussa Firefly Festival (*mid-Jun*). To see one of Japan's classic summer sights, head to Hotaru Park in Fussa, where on the banks of the Tamagawa River hundreds of fireflies are released. There is also street food and stage performances.

SEPTEMBER

△ **Hachiman-gu Festival** (*Sep 14–16*). A procession of floats and horseback archery at the Hachiman-gu shrine in Kamakura draws a big crowd.

Shinagawa Shukuba Matsuri (*last weekend in Sep*). Locals celebrate the rich history of the Shinagwa ward by dressing as samurai, geisha, ninja, and other historical characters.

OCTOBER

△ **The Tokyo Grand Tea Ceremony** (*2nd weekend in Oct*). Taking place in the beautiful Hama-rikyu Gardens, this event gives visitors the chance to try a traditional tea ceremony.

Kanda Used Book Festival (*late Oct*). This is a must for bookworms, as the sidewalks of Yasukuni-dori in Kanda are transformed into a seemingly endless tunnel of books.

MARCH

△ **Hina Matsuri** (*Mar 3*). For Girls' Day, an amazing array of vintage Kyushu dolls are displayed at Meguro Gajoen, a historic hotel.

Golden Dragon Dance (*Mar 18*). Held at Senso-ji temple in Asakusa, this festival celebrates the day 1,400 years ago when two brothers fished a Buddhist statue out of the Sumida River.

APRIL

△ **Cherry blossom season** (*early–mid Apr*). Join hundreds of thousands of Tokyoites and make a beeline for Ueno Park, the perfect place to enjoy *hanami*: the traditional spring picnic gatherings under the cherry blossoms.

Nihonbashi Famous Bridge Spring Festival (*early Apr*). Held to commemorate the construction of the iconic bridge in the Nihonbashi district, this festival recreates the lively spirit of the Edo era.

Buddha's Birthday (*Apr 8*). All over Japan, believers bathe small statues of the Buddha and decorate them with flowers to signify his birth.

JULY

△ **Tanabata** (*Jul 7*). An ancient festival celebrating the annual reunion of the deities Orihime and Hikoboshi. The Japanese mark the occasion by writing wishes on paper and hanging them in trees.

Sumidagawa Fireworks Festival (*last Sat in Jul*). Japan's oldest fireworks festival is held on the banks of the Sumida River in Asakusa.

AUGUST

Obon (*Aug 13–16*). Buddhists across the country visit their family tombs for the festival of the dead, celebrated with lively dances. On the final day, visit Sumida Park to see the Toro Nagashi ceremony, during which people float glowing paper lanterns on the river to commemorate the souls of the dead.

△ **Koenji Awa-Odori** (*last weekend in Aug*). This riotous street festival features some 10,000 performers and more than one million spectators.

NOVEMBER

△ **Tori-no-ichi Festival** (*1–3 days in Nov*). Held on the Day of the Rooster (every 12 days), this festival at Otori Shrine is best enjoyed at night when rows of lanterns cast a golden glow over the street stalls.

Daimyo Gyoretsu (*Nov 3*). Hakone hosts the re-enactment of a feudal lord's procession along the old Tokaido road between Edo and Kyoto.

DECEMBER

Winter Illuminations (*throughout*). At Showa Kinen Park, admire the tall sculptures composed of 15,000 illuminated glass parts each, as well as rows of sparkling trees along the canal.

△ **New Year's Eve** (*Dec 31*). At the stroke of midnight, the lights of Tokyo Tower change color to welcome in the new year, while revelers release strings of balloons.

A BRIEF
HISTORY

Once a sleepy castle town, Edo continued to grow in size and importance over the centuries, becoming the capital of Japan and renamed Tokyo in 1868. Today it is the largest metropolitan area in the world, and a powerhouse of industry, innovation, and creativity.

Edo Transformed

From the founding of the town's first castle in 1170, right up to the late 16th century, the town of Edo was little more than a small fishing settlement. That all changed when Edo was chosen as the headquarters for Tokugawa Ieyasu, a military general who had helped to restore order in Japan following almost a hundred years of warfare between rival feudal lords. Tokugawa became shogun in 1603, closing Japan to most foreign trade and travel in 1633. With the country now at relative peace, Edo boomed, and by the early 1700s the city boasted a population of one million people.

1 A panoramic map of Tokyo, 1883.

2 The landing of Commodore Perry.

3 The Great Kanto Earthquake of 1923.

4 Stamp of Emperor Taisho, the 123rd emperor of Japan.

Timeline of events

c 1170

A warrior of the Edo clan builds a residence in a fishing village at the mouth of the Sumida River.

1457

A samurai governor, Ota Dokan, builds Edo Castle.

1590

Military general Tokugawa Ieyasu is transferred to the Kanto region, establishing himself at Edo.

1603

Tokugawa is named Shogun, beginning the Edo period.

1617

Kabuki, sumo, and ukiyo-e art begin to thrive in Edo culture.

1633

The *sakoku* (closed country) policy begins. Nearly all foreign nationals are barred.

End of Isolation

In 1853 US Navy warships steamed into Edo Bay, and the fleet's commander demanded Japan open itself to trade once more. Weakened by unrest from within, the shogunate acceded to the demands. Lack of support for the shogunate led to a civil war from 1868–9, resulting in the resignation of the shogun and Imperial power being restored. Emperor Meiji moved to Edo, which was renamed Tokyo and became the capital of Japan.

Taisho Tokyo

The reign of Emperor Taisho (1912–1926) saw a vibrant new culture blossom, as young Japanese people reveled in newfound economic, social, and political freedoms. The dynamic era came to a halt when the Great Kanto Earthquake struck the region, and mob violence broke out in the ensuing fires. A crackdown followed: order was restored, individual freedoms curtailed, and laws implemented to end public displays of political dissent. As the city rebuilt, multi-story buildings of concrete and steel were erected in place of the destroyed wooden houses, while new motorways replaced the old twisting narrow streets.

ISOLATIONISM

Sakoku (closed country) was Japan's isolationist foreign policy. It was initiated by the Tokugawa shogunate to promote national stability, and end colonial and religious influence from abroad. From 1633–1853, the Japanese public were not allowed to leave the country, and only the Dutch were allowed to continue trading with Japan.

1657

Great Fire of Meireki occurs in Edo, and over 60 percent of Tokyo is destroyed.

1856

Publication of *One Hundred Famous Views of Edo*, by artist Hiroshige.

1853

Commodore Matthew Perry anchors in Edo Bay and demands an end to Japan's period of isolation.

1868

End of Edo period; Edo city is renamed Tokyo and becomes Japan's new capital.

1923

Great Kanto Earthquake strikes; much of Tokyo and Yokohama are destroyed.

1

2

3

World War II

In December 1941, Japan launched a surprise attack on America's Pacific Fleet in Pearl Harbor, Hawaii. Intended as a preemptive strike to prevent the United States becoming involved in Japan's military affairs in the Pacific, the attack had the opposite effect when it brought the US formally into World War II. The war continued to escalate, and on the night of March 9, 1945, the US Army Air Forces sent 325 B-29s over Tokyo in a devastating firebombing raid. In a matter of minutes more than 100,000 people were dead, and 17 sq miles (45 sq km) of the city had turned to ash. Following the Allies' atomic bombing of the Japanese cities of Hiroshima and Nagasaki in August, Emperor Hirohito ordered the cabinet to sue for peace. The war drew to a close, and was followed by the Allied occupation of Japan.

Rise and Fall

The occupation of Japan finally ended in 1952. The new atmosphere of freedom unleashed a creative shock wave that saw a period of intense innovation in art, film, literature, and architecture – much of this new experimentation happening in the capital city. The success of the 1964 Tokyo Olympic Games

1 Devastating fires following a bombing raid during World War II.

2 The opening of the 1964 Summer Olympics.

3 Shinjuku in 1982.

4 Calligrapher Ryo Fuuka writing "Reiwa."

Did You Know?

During the economic bubble, the Imperial Palace's land was worth more than the state of California.

Timeline of events

1945
Tokyo devastated by Allied firebombing in the final months of World War II.

1946–52
The US Army occupies Japan, with headquarters in Yokohama before moving to Tokyo.

1954
Godzilla rampages through Tokyo for the first time in the movie *Godzilla*.

1964
Tokyo Summer Olympics and Paralympics, the first games held in Asia.

1976
Commercial karaoke machines are introduced in Japan, although they are not very popular at first.

marked Japan's re-entry onto the international stage. The stunning buildings erected to mark the event, and the construction of the first *shinkansen* (bullet train), established Japan's place at the forefront of design and technology. Following decades of intense economic growth, land values skyrocketed in Tokyo in the 1980s. However, this economic bubble came to end in 1992, and years of stagnation followed.

Tokyo Today

The beginning of the 21st century continued to be marked by the difficult aftermath of the bubble burst in the 1990s, as well as the global financial crisis of 2008 and the issues of an aging and declining population. The pessimistic mood of the era was deepened by the 2011 Tohoku Earthquake and subsequent accident at the Fukushima Daiichi Nuclear Power Plant. Nonetheless, throughout these difficult years Tokyo continued to be an important center for art, entertainment, and innovation. With the ascent to the throne of Emperor Naruhito and the dawn of the Reiwa era in 2019, and the thrill of the long-awaited Summer 2020 Olympics, the Japanese are looking eagerly towards the future as Tokyo steps firmly into the spotlight once again.

↑ Tokyo Tower celebrating Tokyo's winning bid for the 2020 Olympic Games.

1995
Aum Shinrikyo cult releases sarin gas on three lines of the Tokyo Metro.

1998
Tokyo gets its first Pokémon Center, a store dedicated to Japan's hit video game and anime franchise.

2012
Opening of the Tokyo Skytree, the world's tallest tower.

2019
Emperor Naruhito ascends the throne, ushering in the new Reiwa era.

2020
Tokyo Summer Olympic and Paralympic Games.

EXPERIENCE

A busy street in eastern Shinjuku

Mirror-encased escalator at Tokyu Plaza Omotesando Harajuku mall

WESTERN TOKYO

Shinjuku and Shibuya, the dual centers of Western Tokyo, three stops apart on the Yamanote Line, started to boom only after the 1923 earthquake and the opening of the Tokyu Toyoko line, linking the capital and Yokohama, in 1923. Despite its short history, the area still has stories to tell, from Hachiko – the dog who faithfully waited for his owner outside Shibuya Station everyday from 1924 to 1935 – to the US occupation of Yoyogi Park between 1946 and 1964. The park remained on the world stage for the 1964 Summer Olympic and Paralympic Games.

This part of the city is new Tokyo – all vitality and energy, fast-paced, constantly changing, and challenging the more traditional pleasures of Central and Northern Tokyo. When the Imperial Japanese Army moved to Roppongi in 1890, the area became a nightlife hot spot, and this reputation was only reinforced with the influx of expatriates after World War II. Although it is no longer burdened with a sleazy reputation, people still flock here after dark for Roppongi's cosmopolitan clubs, bars, and music venues, and the neon lights and *pachinko* parlors of East Shinjuku. On top of this, Shibuya, along with neighboring Harajuku and Minami-Aoyama, have been the epicenters of both young and haute-couture Japanese fashion since the 1980s.

WESTERN TOKYO

Must Sees
❶ Meiji Shrine
❷ West Shinjuku
❸ Roppongi
❹ Harajuku

Experience More
❺ Shinjuku Station
❻ Minami-Aoyama
❼ Tokyo Opera City
❽ Shibuya Crossing
❾ Bunka Gakuen Costume Museum
❿ Samurai Museum
⓫ Yoyogi Park
⓬ Akasaka

Eat
① Maruhachi
② Den

Drink
③ New York Bar

Stay
④ Hotel Beat Wave
⑤ The Millennials Shibuya

Shop
⑥ Shibuya 109

MEIJI SHRINE

明治神宮

C7 **1-1 Yoyogikamizonocho** **Harajuku** **Treasure Museum and Annex: closed for renovation; Naien inner precinct: dawn to dusk daily (times vary seasonally)** **meijijingu.or.jp**

For Tokyo's residents, the lush 170-acre (69-ha) grounds of the Meiji Shrine (Meiji Jingu) are a welcome green lung in the heart of this hectic city. As the capital's most important Shinto shrine, it offers visitors a tantalizing glimpse of an older Japan. Take a stroll through its beautiful grounds, stocked with some 120,000 trees, learn more about the imperial family through the artifacts on display in the museums, and soak up traditional temple life.

Originally built in 1920, the Meiji Shrine was destroyed during World War II in an air raid, but was rebuilt in 1958. Controversially, the shrine was rededicated to Emperor Meiji (1852–1912), rather than a *kami* (spirit), contravening the imperial family's reuninciation of divinity in 1946. At the Treasure Museum and its annex, visitors can see items belonging to the imperial family, including gorgeous kimonos, lacquerware, and furniture. Don't miss the shrine's inner precinct (Naien), said to have been designed by Emperor Meiji for his wife. Here, a teahouse overlooks a pond stocked with water lilies and carp. To the right of the pond, a path leads to the beautiful Minami-ike Shobuda (iris garden), containing over 150 species.

Guiding Spirit

One of the most striking sights at the Meiji Shrine is the huge wall of sake barrels. While the barrels on display are empty, they are loaded with meaning. Sake is supposed to facilitate the connection with the gods and in the oldest Japanese texts "miki," the old word for sake, is written with the characters for "god" and "wine." Shinto shrines pray for the brewers' prosperity and, in turn, the breweries donate sake for the shrines' rituals and ceremonies.

THE MEIJI EMPEROR

Having succeeded to the throne in 1868 at just 14 years of age, the Meiji Emperor set out to modernize Japan. During his reign, the Diet was founded, the industrial revolution took place, and the country emerged victorious from conflicts with China, Korea, and Russia.

> ### PICTURE PERFECT
> **Here Comes the Bride**
>
> Fortunate visitors may catch a glimpse of a traditional Shinto wedding taking place at the shrine. Take a picture of the bride in her magnificent wedding kimono (from a respectful distance), as she shelters under a red parasol accompanied by a procession of priests.

←
Visitors performing *harai* (ritual cleansing) before approaching the shrine

→
Admiring the huge wall of empty sake barrels, marked with the name of the breweries they were made in, at the entrance to the shrine

↑ Visitors at the Minami-shin Mon, the gate to Meiji Shrine's inner sanctuary

②

WEST SHINJUKU

西新宿

B5 **&** Shinjuku

Many of Tokyo's skyscraper office blocks (and some of its most expensive land) are clustered just to the west of Shinjuku Station. About 250,000 people work here each day, creating endless bustle. Many of west Shinjuku's hotels, and some of its office blocks, have top-floor restaurants or observation areas with views of the city.

In 1960 the government designated Shinjuku a *fukutoshin* ("secondary heart of the city"), and in 1991, when the city government moved into architect Kenzo Tange's massive 48-story Metropolitan Government Offices, many started calling it *shin toshin* (the new capital). Tange's building was dubbed "tax tower" by those outraged at its US$1 billion cost. Between the skyscrapers, the streets pulsate with people shopping, heading to restaurants, and seeking evening entertainment, including *pachinko* parlours, nightclubs, and love hotels.

↑ Observation deck on the 45th floor of the Tokyo Metropolitan Government Offices

Did You Know?

Shoppers spend over ¥1.3 trillion in Shinjuku's stores every year.

Hilton Tokyo

Dai-Ichi Seimei Building

Hyatt Regency Tokyo

The Tokyo Metropolitan Government Offices' observatory grants views of Mount Fuji and Tokyo Bay on clear days.

Shinjuku Central Park

→ The towering skyscrapers of West Shinjuku

DRINK

New York Bar

The Park Hyatt Tokyo hotel will be forever linked to Sofia Coppola's 2003 film *Lost in Translation*. There is no better spot in Tokyo than this iconic bar to order a whisky soda, while gazing out at Tokyo's twinkling lights.

🅿 B6 🏢 52 Fl, Park Hyatt Tokyo, 3-7-1-2, Nishishinjuku ⏰ 5pm-1am Thu-Sat, 5pm-midnight Sun-Wed 🆆 tokyo.park. hyatt.co.jp

Island Tower

Visit the Sumitomo Building's observatory for free.

Nomura Building

Mitsui Building

Sonpo Japan Building

Shinjuku Center Building

Keio Plaza Hotel

The Monolith Building has a pleasant courtyard garden on the north side.

KDDI Building

The Washington Hotel has flowing curves and tiny windows on its white facade.

↑ The distinctive Sonpo Japan Building, with its graceful curving base

③

ROPPONGI

六本木

⑨E5 ⑤Roppongi

The buzzing neighborhood of Roppongi is where Tokyo's grownups come to play. Once famous for its dissolute nightlife, the district has been transformed by the appearance of several major art galleries and the huge investment in Roppongi Hills. Today Roppongi is a draw as much for its culture, shopping, and entertainment as it is for its still vibrant clubbing scene.

Roppongi Hills

 roppongihills.com

Opened in 2003, this chic commercial and residential complex is one of the largest developments of its kind in Japan. The stunning mix of upmarket restaurants, bars, cafés, shops, museums, and entertainment venues all bound together in a cutting-edge architectural vision, makes it easy to spend an entire day in this enormous complex. The area is also sprinkled with fascinating outdoor art installations and beautiful green areas that complement the indoor artistic spaces, and provide plenty of places to take a break as you explore the complex.

Roppongi Hills can often feel like it has a more cosmopolitan vibe than some other entertainment districts in the city, as it is a popular nightlife and shopping spot for Tokyo's international community.

---

②

Mori Art Museum

⚑Roppongi Hills Mori Tower, 6-10-1 Roppongi, Minato ⏱10am–10pm daily (to 5pm Tue) ⓦmori.art.museum

Immerse yourself in Roppongi Hill's renowned art scene with a visit to the Mori Art Museum, located in the stunning Mori Tower. This is one of three art spaces that comprises the "Roppongi Art Triangle", along with the National Art Center Tokyo and the Suntory Museum of Art.

The glamorous space features constantly rotating exhibitions, with a focus on contemporary pieces and the postwar avant-garde. The museum has become an influential presence within Japan's art scene, renowned for showcasing the hottest artists, such as Takashi Murakami and Leandro Erlich.

The Mori Tower contains several other attractions worth visiting. The **Mori Arts Center Gallery** hosts short-term exhibitions on various themes, from historical figures to manga and anime. The tower's two observation areas – **Tokyo City View** and **Rooftop Sky Deck** – offer incredible panoramas over the capital, with the latter also hosting star-gazing parties on the open-air rooftop.

Mori Arts Center Gallery
 ⏱10am–8pm daily
ⓦmacg.roppongihills.com

Tokyo City View
 ⏱10am–11pm Mon–Thu, 10am–1am Fri & Sat ⓦtcv.roppongihills.com/en/index.html

↑ Overlooking the city from the Rooftop Sky Deck on Mori Tower

MINAMI-AOYAMA

Nogi Shrine ③

GAIEN - HIGASHI - DORI

AKASAKA - DORI

AKASAKA

21_21 Design Sight

Hinokicho Park

Toraya
Tokyo Midtown

Nogizaka S

Suntory Museum of Art ⑦

Tokyo Midtown ⑤

⑥ Fujifilm Square

④

The National Art Center, Tokyo

Roppongi S

ROPPONGI-DORI

GAIEN - HIGASHI - DORI

EXPRESSWAY NO. 3

ROPPONGI

ROPPONGI-DORI

GAIEN - NISHI-DORI

TV ASAHI - DORI

Mori Art Museum ②

① Roppongi Hills

Toho Cinema

NISHI-AZABU

Grand Hyatt

0 meters 400
0 yards 400

N ↑

Rooftop Sky Deck
♿ ⏰ 11am–8pm daily
🌐 tcv.roppongihills.com/en/index.html

---

③
Nogi Shrine

🏠 8-Chome-11-27 Akasaka, Minato ⏰ Early–6pm daily 🌐 nogijinja.or.jp

Nogi Shrine is dedicated to General Nogi Maresuke and his wife Shizuko. General Nogi was a hero in Imperial-era Japan, famous for his intense loyalty and personal honor. When Emperor Meiji died in 1912, the couple decided to demonstrate their loyalty to the deceased emperor and commitment to old-fashioned samurai values. On the day of the Emperor's funeral, the couple committed the ritual, suicide act of seppuku (disembowelment).

Despite the violent nature of their end, the shrine dedicated to General Nogi and Shizuko is a beautiful place, and an oasis of tranquility and tradition amid the rest of the bustling, modern Roppongi district.

In the adjacent gardens of Nogi Park, the Nogi family's 19th century house still remains, unharmed during both the Great Kanto Earthquake (1923) and World War II. The house is open to visitors on the eve and anniversary of the couple's death on September 12–13, and can be seen in the gardens throughout the year. There is also a flea market held in the shrine's grounds on the fourth Saturday of each month (weather permitting).

↑ Louise Bourgeois's *Maman* (1999) outside the Mori Art Museum

PICTURE PERFECT
Not so Itsy Bitsy

Head to the Mori Art Museum to see Louise Bourgeois's spider-like *Maman*. At a terrifying 30 ft (9 m) tall and 33 ft (10 m) wide, the bronze statue is the stuff of nightmares. Pose next to one of the sculpture's towering legs to show the perspective.

→ An art installation by Kengo Kito at the National Art Center, Tokyo *(inset)*

④ 🖉 🍴 🖥 🛍

The National Art Center, Tokyo

🏠 **7 Chome-22-2 Roppongi, Minato** ⏰ **Times vary, check website** 🌐 **nact.jp**

Another point of the Roppongi Art Triangle, the National Art Center, Tokyo (NACT) was built in 2007 as part of an effort to reinvent Roppongi as something more than just a nightlife hub. The work of renowned Metabolist architect Kisho Kurokawa, the rippling glass facade of the building was inspired by waves and hills. One of Japan's largest exhibition spaces, the NACT does not have a permanent collection of its own, but focuses entirely on special temporary exhibitions, artist associations' displays, and educational programs. Check the NACT website to see what incredible offerings are held during your trip.

⑤ 🖉 🖥 🛍

Tokyo Midtown

🏠 **Tokyo Midtown Galleria, 9-7-4 Akasaka, Minato** 🌐 **tokyo-midtown.com**

Completed in 2007, this high-rise development helped spur Roppongi's transformation into a chic district for shopping, entertainment, and art. Similar to the nearby Roppongi Hills *(p68)*, Tokyo Midtown is full of stores, eateries, and museums in the Galleria, Plaza and Midtown Tower buildings, and is bordered to the northeast by the vast and sculpture-filled Hinokicho Park. This beautiful park is located on the former site of the gardens belonging to the lords of the Hagi clan, and harks back to the time when Roppongi was covered in cypress trees *(hinoki)*.

Opposite the park is the **21_21 Design Sight** gallery, a collaboration by architect Tadao Ando and fashion designer Issey Miyake, with the goal to enrich everyday life through the beauty of thoughtful design. The fascinating and unique exhibits change regularly, and the museum store is like a gallery of its own.

21_21 Design Sight

🖉 🖥 🛍 ⏰ **10am–8pm daily** 🌐 **macg.roppongihills.com**

⑥

Fujifilm Square

🏠 **9-Chome-7-3 Akasaka, Minato** ⏰ **10am–7pm daily** 🌐 **fujifilmsquare.jp**

For a fun, free activity in Roppongi, check out this gallery space by the Fuji company. The Photo Salon showcases photos from the Japanese Meiji era to the present day, while Touch Fujifilm lets visitors try out all the latest cameras and tech.

Did You Know?

Midtown Tower is the second tallest building in Tokyo (after Tokyo Skytree). It's the fifth tallest in Japan.

⑦

Suntory Museum of Art

🏠 Tokyo Midtown Galleria, 9-7-4 Akasaka, Minato
🕐 10am–6pm daily (to 8pm Fri–Sat) 🌐 suntory.co.jp/sma

The third and final point of the Roppongi Art Triangle is inside the Tokyo Midtown Galleria. Here, the Suntory

Museum of Art showcases the collection of the Suntory company, which has amassed a fortune producing whisky and beer. In contrast to the other two museums in the Triangle, Suntory's exhibits focus on older works and traditional crafts, hosting a series of changing exhibitions on textiles, glass, lacquerware, and ceramics.

Embracing the traditional spirit of the exhibits, the museum also hosts tea ceremonies every other Thursday, in a beautifully tranquil and traditional tea ceremony room with tatami mat floors. Reservations are not available, so be sure to buy your ticket early on the day (available from 10am at the museum's reception desk).

←

Elaborately decorated plates on display in the Suntory Museum of Art

SHOP

Toraya Tokyo Midtown

Founded around 500 years ago, Toraya is Japan's leading producer of *wagashi* (traditional sweets). These delicacies are most often presented as elegant gifts when visiting friends, and seasonal sweets are enjoyed during tea ceremonies. The Roppongi branch houses a shop, tea room, and gallery where visitors can learn about the history of *wagashi*.

🏠 D-B117, 9-7-4 Akasaka, Minato
🕐 11am–9pm daily
🌐 toraya-group.co.jp

4

HARAJUKU

原宿

📍 C8 🚇 Harajuku 🚇 Meiji-jingumae, Omotesando

Harajuku Station was the main station for the 1964 Tokyo Olympic village, and the concentration of international culture had a great impact on the area, attracting young and innovative Tokyoites. Over the following decades, Harajuku evolved into a thriving fashion district, teeming with both high-end international brands and independent boutiques.

 ①

Takeshita-dori

This is Harajuku's go-to shopping street, with stores epitomizing the district's bold, expressive fashion culture. Sundays bring the biggest crowds, so be prepared for a long parade of pedestrians – although people-watching is half the fun here.

Interspersed among the boutiques are a few stores dedicated entirely to *puri-kura*. These photo booths create flattering pictures, and can be decorated with stamps, writing, and colorful backgrounds. For many Japanese teens, it's tradition to take pictures in these booths during any outing with friends, so jump in for a cheap, classic Harajuku souvenir.

---

 ②

Togo Shrine

📷 1-5-3 Jingumae 🌐 harajukutogo.wixsite.com/togojinja

This small shrine, located in a quiet, tree-filled area off Takeshita-dori, is a good

↑ Crowds on neon-lit Takeshita-dori, in the Harajuku District

example of what makes Shinto so unique. The *kami* (divine spirit) celebrated here is Admiral Togo, who defeated the Russian fleet in the 1905 Russo-Japanese War.

TOP 3 **LUXURY SHOPPING SPOTS**

Omotesando
📷 5-7 Jingumae
A boulevard lined with upmarket boutiques such as Chanel and Dior.

Omotesando Hills
📷 4-12-10 Jingumae
🌐 omotesandohills.com
100 shops, restaurants, and cafés including international greats and local designers.

Oak Omotesando
📷 3-6-1 Kita Aoyama
🌐 oakomotesando.com
A glass building housing several luxury brands.

PICTURE PERFECT
Japan in the Mirror

Quirky Tokyu Plaza Omotesando Harajuku, a multi-story shopping complex in the heart of the district, is accessed via a mirror-encased escalator *(p60)*. Snap a kaleidoscope-like image from the top as you exit.

③
Cat Street

This quiet area of Harajuku is the place to seek out the very latest trends. Stores here sell affordable creations by local designers, exclusive items from high-end international brands, and even vintage clothes. Don't forget to check out the maze of alleyways branching off the main street.

④
Laforet

⌂ 11-11-6 Jinguma ⏰ 11am–9pm daily ⓦ laforet.ne.jp

Quintessentially Harajuku in spirit, this department store is particularly good for women's casual wear, from Vivienne Westwood to local indie brands, and gets packed during its biannual Grand Bazar Sale in July and January.

⑤ ▭
Design Festa Gallery

⌂ West Bldg, 3-20-18 Jingumae ⏰ 11am–8pm daily ⓦ designfesta gallery.com

A striking white building enveloped in black steel pipes, this gallery has 21 show rooms packed with amazing art.

⑥ ⟨⟩ ⌂
Ota Memorial Museum of Art

⌂ 1-10-10 Jingumae ⏰ 10:30am–5:30pm Tue-Sun ⓒ For exhibit changes, check website for details ⓦ ukiyo-e-ota-muse.jp

A treasure trove for lovers of ukiyo-e *(p150)*, this museum has a collection of over 12,000 prints from different eras. The works on display are changed every month according to different themes.

HARAJUKU STYLE

Harajuku has been a mecca for Tokyo teens since the mid-1990s, when disparate fashion sub-cultures would gather near the former Olympic Park to shop. At the time, a magazine called *FRUiTS* would feature portraits of young people in zany outfits, popularizing the idea of Tokyo as a hub for teen fashion. A number of mainstream brands moved into the district, transforming it into a tourist hot spot. The print edition of *FRUiTS* ceased publication in 2017, but one Sunday a month, devotees still gather for the Harajuku Fashion Walk to relive the glory days.

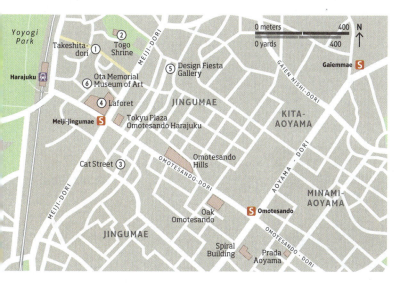

↑ Commuters on the platform at Shinjuku, the busiest train station in the world

EXPERIENCE MORE

5

Shinjuku Station
新宿駅

 C5 🚃🚇 Ⓦ shinjukustation.com

With over two million people passing through each day, this is the world's busiest train station. A major stop on both the JR and metropolitan subway systems, Shinjuku Station is also the starting point for trains and buses into the suburbs. On the Yamanote and Chuo line platforms during the morning rush hour (about 7:30–9am), staff are employed to firmly push those last few commuters on to the train.

It is easy to lose your way in the maze of seemingly identical passages between the lines. For a time in the 1980s and early 1990s, a substantial number of homeless people built cardboard villages in the station's corridors. In a controversial move, the municipal government forcibly removed them to less visible areas.

> ### COMMUTER CULTURE
>
> Commuters packed into trains are a common sight in Tokyo. High house prices force people farther out of the city, and a commute of at least an hour is standard. An entire industry has come up around commuters, including stand-up eateries serving meals to those with a long ride ahead.

6

Minami-Aoyama
南青山

 D9 🚇 Gaienmae, Omotesando, Nogizaka, Aoyama-itchome

Favored by artists and young entrepreneurs, this neighborhood encompasses the area to the south of Aoyama-dori street, between Aoyama Cemetery and Shibuya. There are many fashionable places to explore here, especially Aoyama-dori itself: a wide street that has become a center for boutiques and upscale life.

On Gaien-Nishi-dori is the **Watari-um** (Watari Museum of Contemporary Art). Exhibits are by international and Japanese artists, and change regularly. Back on Aoyama-dori, turn left at the Omotesando junction for the **Nezu Museum**, which houses a collection of Korean, Chinese, and Japanese art and is situated in landscaped gardens containing traditional teahouses. You will find a very different museum a few blocks away. The **Taro Okamoto Memorial Museum** houses the peculiar works of post-war sculptor Taro Okamoto (1911–96). The towering figures have crudely

> ### Did You Know?
>
> Tokyo's crows know how to use tools and can recognize human faces.

INSIDER TIP

INSIDER TIP
Take the Bus

At Shinjuku Station South you'll find the Expressway Bus Terminal, giving access to Japan's incredible coach system. For travellers on a budget, the overnight buses are a great alternative to the rail network. Book a bus at the terminal or online (*www.shinjuku-busterminal.co.jp*).

realized faces and tapering plant-like tendrils.

A short walk from here is Kotto-dori, which is full of antique shops selling scrolls, paintings, and porcelain. This street is one of the hottest in Tokyo, with some notable boutiques, cafés, and shops.

Return to Aoyama-dori, near the Omotesando junction toward Shibuya, and the next landmark you come to is the white, geometric Spiral Building, which owes its name to the large spiral ramp inside. Designed by Fumihiko Maki in 1985, it is one of the most popular places in Minami-Aoyama. There is nothing in it that cannot be described as trendy (*torendi* in Japanese), and that includes most of the people. Attractions comprise a first-floor exhibition and performance space, the Spiral Hall, also used for exhibitions and performances, an Italian café, a French restaurant, a house-wares boutique, and a beauty salon. Spiral even has its own record label focusing on jazz and world music.

Head eastward toward the Nogizaka subway station for the **Aoyama Cemetery**, Japan's first public necropolis, and probably its most exclusive.

→

An upscale boutique near Omotesando, in Minami-Aoyama

A number of high-profile Japanese are buried here, including former prime minister Shigeru Yoshida and famed novelist Yukio Mishima. This tranquil, green spot is also a popular place to view cherry blossoms.

Watari-um
⊛ ⊜ 🏠 3-7-6 Jingumae
🕙 11am–7pm Tue–Sun (to 9pm Wed) 🌐 watarium.co.jp

Nezu Museum
⊛ 🏠 6-5-1 Minamiaoyama
🕙 10am–5pm Tue–Sun
🌐 nezu-muse.or.jp

Taro Okamoto Memorial Museum
⊛ 🏠 6-1-19 Minamiaoyama
🕙 10am–6pm Wed–Mon
🌐 taro-okamoto.or.jp

Aoyama Cemetery
⊛ 🏠 2-32-2 Minato 📞 (03) 3401-3652 🕙 24 hours daily

STAY

Hotel Beat Wave
This music-themed option on "Love Hotel Hill" has karaoke machines in every room.

📍 B10 🏠 2-9 Maruyamachō, Shibuya
🌐 beatwave.co.jp

¥¥¥

The Millennials Shibuya
Free beer is served for one hour every evening at this sociable capsule hotel.

📍 C9 🏠 1-20-13 Jinnan, Shibuya 🌐 the-millennials.jp/shibuya

¥¥¥

7 🍴 🖥 🛍

Tokyo Opera City
東京オペラシティー

📍 A6 🏢 3-20-2 Nishi-Shinjuku, Shinjuku 🚇 Hatsudai 🌐 operacity.jp

This towering skyscraper is home to Tokyo's impressive music and theater complex. On the first floor of the building, you'll find two main halls. One of these is used primarily for Japanese classical music and theater, while the second is a vast opera hall with a soaring vaulted roof that stages large-scale opera recitals. Performances are frequent – check the calendar on Opera City's website for up-to-date listings, and book your tickets in advance.

On top of the two halls there are 54 floors, mostly housing company offices. The first three floors are accessible to the public, however, and house an art gallery, shops, and restaurants, which are worth investigating before or after the opera. The expansive NTT Intercommunication Center occupies the fourth floor. This is one of Tokyo's primary centers for modern interactive art. The 53rd and 54th floors of the buildings hold a dozen restaurants and bars, some of which boast great city views.

 PICTURE PERFECT
Walk this Way

The second floor of the glass-fronted Starbucks at Shibuya Tsutaya is the perfect place to get a shot of the famous Shibuya Crossing – the busiest intersection in the world. Grab a coffee before making a beeline for the second floor, where the window seats offer great views of the madness below.

8

Shibuya Crossing
渋谷スクランブル

📍 C10 🏢 1–22, Shibuya 🚉 & Ⓢ & 🚌 Shibuya

If visitors had to pick one defining view of Tokyo, Shibuya Crossing would be a leading contender. Also kown as the Shibuya Scramble, the crossing is located outside the major transport hub of Shibuya Station, which sees 2.4 million passengers a day. At peak times, more than 2,500 people cross the road from five different directions each time the light goes green.

This area is where Japan's youth come to party, and the mass of billboards, lights, and enormous television screens blaring out adverts has made the crossing the defining image of the city. The cafés and restaurants that look

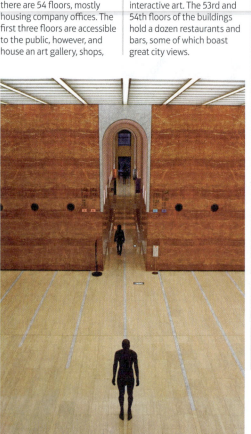

← The art gallery at the Tokyo Opera City, one of the city's major exhibition spaces

← Crowds of pedestrians using the famous Shibuya Crossing

500,000

The number of people who use Shibuya Crossing every day – up to 2,500 at a time.

down at the intersection from the buildings that surround it can feel almost as busy as the Shibuya Scramble itself, as hundreds of people vie for window space to try and photograph the crossing.

⑨

Bunka Gakuen Costume Museum
歌舞伎座

📍 B6 📞 (03) 3299-2387 🚉 & Ⓢ Shinjuku 🕐 10am-4:30pm Mon-Sat

Opened in 1979, the museum has been building up its collection of costumes and accessories to the over 20,000 exhibits that it holds today.

Clothing and dyed articles from such countries and regions as Africa, the Middle East, China, and India are exhibited throughout the year. Western attire is also represented; on display is a selection of dresses typifying fashions of the 18th to 20th centuries. Among the permanent items of interest in the Japanese collection are modern court dresses, or *kosode* (short-sleeved kimonos), the lavish costumes worn for Noh dramas, and a collection of bags. The museum also exhibits the creations of Japanese haute couture designers.

SHOP

Shibuya 109
This department store located alongside the famous Shibuya Crossing is an icon of cool, youthful Japanese fashion culture.

📍 C10 🏠 2 Chome-29-1 Dogenzaka 🕐 10am-9pm daily 🚫 Jan 1 🌐 shibuya109.jp

↑ Displays of 18th-century Western dress at the Bunka Gakuen Costume Museum

Crowds teeming across Shibuya Crossing

Elaborate samurai armor on display in the Samurai Museum in Kabukicho

Samurai Museum
サムライミュージアム

📍C5 🏠2-25-6 Kabukicho, Shinjuku 🚉Seibu-Shinjuku 🚇&🚇Shinjuku ⏰10:30am–9pm daily 🌐samurai museum.jp

Geared toward international visitors and conveniently located in Kabukicho, this museum displays samurai swords, armor, and a plethora of other fearsome-looking weapons. Its beautifully laid-out displays put the rise of the samurai in context and explain the history of this uniquely Japanese style of warfare, as well as what happened when the Japanese

EATING IN GOLDEN GAI

Just around the corner from the Samurai Museum, the Golden Gai area retains a shabby charm that is fast disappearing in the increasingly slick and tidy modern city. In this labyrinth of dark alleys and backlit acrylic signs, there are more than 200 tiny bars and restaurants to choose from. But don't head over too early – nothing opens before 9pm. Plus, there's no rush, as the fun goes on all night.

warriors came up against the Mongols in the 13th century.

Visitors can indulge in some Japanese-style cosplay, try on lacquered armor, and handle a reproduction *katana* sword. Enthusiastic English-speaking guides give regular tours that include demonstrations of sword moves and terrifying battle cries. Exhibition fights are regularly staged. Calligraphy classes are also held.

To see some more amazing suits of armor, head to the Tokyo National Museum in Ueno Park *(p114)*.

Yoyogi Park
代々木公園

📍B8 🚉Harajuku, Sangubashi 🚇Yoyogi-koen

For almost three decades the park filled with performers and bands every Sunday. These events were stopped by the authorities in the mid-1990s, supposedly owing to worries about maintaining public order. Weekends are still a good time to visit – for the occasional flea markets and an array of annual events, such as international food festivals and Earth Day. At the entrance to the park you can still see members of the *zoku* (tribes) who used to perform here, from punks and goths to hippies and break-dancers.

Kenzo Tange's two Olympic stadiums, the landmark

structures in Yoyogi Park, were completed in 1964 for the Tokyo Olympics. They are currently being renovated for the upcoming 2020 Tokyo Olympics, when they will be used as handball venues and for wheelchair rugby in the Paralympics. The impressive curves of the shell-like structures are achieved with the use of steel suspension cables.

Akasaka
赤坂

📍F8 🚇Akasaka, Akasaka-Mitsuke

With the Diet Building *(p102)* and many government offices just to the east, Akasaka is a

TOP 5 SYMBOLIC ANIMALS

Fox
Messengers of Shinto god Inari, fox statues are found at shrines.

Cranes
Cranes represent longevity. Japanese folklore says that they live for 1,000 years.

Tanuki
Sculptures of these Asian raccoon dogs represent good luck.

Cats
The Maneki-neko (beckoning cat) is thought to bring luck, wealth, and prosperity.

Koi
Carp symbolize faithfulness and marriage in Japan.

favorite place for politicians to socialize. The roads are often dotted with limousines ferrying men and women to the many exclusive establishments lining the streets here.

Near Akasaka-Mitsuke Station is Toyokawa Inari Shrine (also called Myogon-ji). With its red lanterns and flags, and dozens of statues of foxes (the traditional messengers of Inari, a Shinto deity), this is a pleasant place to linger for a while. While exploring the area you may also see a large building that was featured in the James Bond film *You Only Live Twice* (1967). This is the huge, luxurious Hotel New Otani. On the 17th floor is THE SKY revolving restaurant, which which offers stunning 360-degree views across central Tokyo and the Imperial Palace (p98). In the vast grounds is a magnificent 17th-century Japanese garden, which is free to enter. To the west of Hotel New Otani is a surprising Tokyo landmark: the grand Akasaka Palace (also known as the State Guesthouse), which was modeled after the palaces of Europe. Built in 1909 as a residence for the Imperial family, it is now used as accommodation for visiting dignitaries to Tokyo.

South of Akasaka-Mitsuke Station is the shrine of Hie Jinja, which was erected in 1478. In mid-June, the Sanno Matsuri is celebrated here with a grand procession of 50 *mikoshi* (portable shrines) and people dressed in costumes of the Heian era (794–1185).

The approach to Toyokawa Inari Shrine in the Akasaka District, lined by dozens of fox statues *(inset)*

EAT

Maruhachi
The food served at this friendly *izakaya* can be washed down with *shochu*, a 20–25% spirit usually made with rice or sweet potato.

📍 B10 🏠 2-10-12 Dogenzaka, Shibuya 📞 (03) 3476-5739

Den
Chef Zaiyu Hasegawa crafts beautiful dishes. Order the "Dentucky Fried Chicken."

📍 D8 🏠 2-3-18 Jingumae, Shibuya 🕐 Lunch & Sun 🌐 jimbochoden.com

A SHORT WALK
EAST SHINJUKU

Distance 1.5 miles (2.5 km) **Time** 35 minutes
Nearest subway Shinjuku Station

The eastern part of the Shinjuku district is where Tokyoites come to play. The area has been a nightlife center since Edo times, when it was the first night stop on the old Tokaido road to Kyoto (the capital of Japan at the time). Since Shinjuku Station (p74) opened in the 19th century, entertainment in the area has been targeted at evening commuters (mainly men) en route back to the suburbs. Amusements are focused in the tiny bars of Golden Gai (p80) and in the red-light district of Kabukicho. Daytime attractions include several art galleries, a tranquil shrine, and some department stores. Take a late-afternoon stroll as the neon starts to light up.

Did You Know?

Despite its name, a Kabuki theater was never built in Kabukicho.

Instantly recognizable by its huge TV screen, **Studio Alta** *is a popular place for meeting up or just hanging out.*

Blue Bottle Coffee *is a convenient stop.*

Seibu-shinjuku

CINECITY SQUARE

OTAKIBASHI-DORI

GINZA-DORI

KABUKICHO

CHUO-DORI

START

MOA 2ND ST

MOA CHUO

Studio Alta

MOA 3RD

FINISH

Shinjuku Station

Blue Bottle Coffee

0 meters 150
0 yards 150

N

↑ Flashing advertisements on the exterior of Studio Alta shopping complex

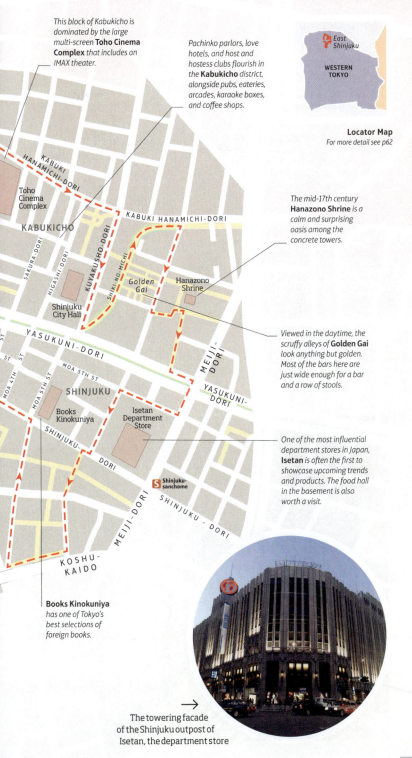

This block of Kabukicho is dominated by the large multi-screen **Toho Cinema Complex** that includes an IMAX theater.

Pachinko parlors, love hotels, and host and hostess clubs flourish in the **Kabukicho** district, alongside pubs, eateries, arcades, karaoke boxes, and coffee shops.

East Shinjuku

WESTERN TOKYO

Locator Map
For more detail see p62

Toho Cinema Complex

KABUKICHO

KABUKI HANAMICHI-DORI

KABUKI HANAMICHI-DORI

SAKURA-DORI

HIGASHI-DORI

KUYAKUSHO-DORI

SHIKI-NO-MICHI

Golden Gai

Hanazono Shrine

Shinjuku City Hall

The mid-17th century **Hanazono Shrine** is a calm and surprising oasis among the concrete towers.

YASUKUNI-DORI

MOA 5TH ST

MOA 4TH ST

MOA 5TH ST

SHINJUKU

MEIJI-DORI

YASUKUNI-DORI

Viewed in the daytime, the scruffy alleys of **Golden Gai** look anything but golden. Most of the bars here are just wide enough for a bar and a row of stools.

Books Kinokuniya

Isetan Department Store

SHINJUKU-DORI

S Shinjuku-sanchome

SHINJUKU - DORI

One of the most influential department stores in Japan, **Isetan** is often the first to showcase upcoming trends and products. The food hall in the basement is also worth a visit.

MEIJI-DORI

SHINJUKU - DORI

KOSHU-KAIDO

Books Kinokuniya *has one of Tokyo's best selections of foreign books.*

→ The towering facade of the Shinjuku outpost of Isetan, the department store

A SHORT WALK
SHIBUYA

Distance 1.5 miles (2.5 km) **Time** 35 minutes
Nearest subway Shibuya Station

Shibuya has been the *sakariba* (party town) for Tokyo's youth since the 1930s, when the Tokyu Toyoko Line made the area a key terminal between the capital and Yokohama, and the first facades featured rockets streaking across the sky. Today it still feels out of this world and cutting edge, and this is where you'll find the latest in fashion and music.

Shibuya's continuing expansion has been spurred by the appetites of the increasingly affluent youth of the world's third-biggest economy. Due to their demands, the area – which lies to the northwest of Shibuya Station and south of Yoyogi Park – is a mix of trendy boutiques, fashionable department stores, and record shops, especially in the vicinity of the iconic Shibuya Crossing *(p76)*, used by thousands of pedestrians every day. On top of these commercial enterprises, a stroll through the area will also take you past a couple of interesting museums, and the Bunkamura cultural center. Once you've explored Shibuya, head into the adjoining area of Dogen-zaka, where you'll find a jumble of sloping streets and alleyways lined with nightclubs, bars, and love hotels.

Did You Know?

Pachinko is similar to pinball. The goal is to collect steel balls, which are exchanged for prizes.

Bunkamura *is a popular site for rock and classical concerts, but also shows movies and has an art gallery and a theater.*

INOKASHIRA-DORI

SHOTO

Bunkamura

Tsutaya O-East

Yosano Akiko Monument

Live musicians perform at **Tsutaya O-East** *every night.*

The **Yosano Akiko Monument** *immortalizes the female poet.*

← Nighttime traffic on an expressway in Shibuya

This purple clock tower stands in front of the Shibuya Ward Office and is overlooked by Yoyogi Park and the NHK Studios.

The Humax Pavilion, resembling a cartoon rocket, is one of the most fanciful buildings in the area.

Locator Map
For more detail see p62

WESTERN TOKYO

Shibuya

0 meters 200
0 yards 200

N

Clock Tower

UDAGAWACHO

Jingu-dori Park

JINNAN

KOEN - DORI

ORGAN - ZAKA

Tokyu Hands

PENGUIN ST

KOEN - DORI

Miyashita Park

Tower Records *has a good stock of Japanese and international music.*

Tower Records

Marui Department Store *is a paradise for clothes – the place for fashionable under 25s.*

Humax Pavilion

Marui Jam

PARK ST

MEIJI - DORI

INOKASHIRA - DORI

SHIBUYA CENTER GAI

Center Gai *is lined with shops, pachinko parlors, restaurants, and karaoke bars full of students.*

BUNKAMURA - DORI

START/ FINISH

SHIBUYA

Shibuya 109 Building

DOGEN - ZAKA

Statue of Hachiko

Shibuya Mark City

Shibuya Station

The **Statue of Hachiko** *has stood here since 1934, commemorating the dog who waited for his master at the station every night for more than a decade after his death.*

Shibuya bus station

DOGENZAKA

TAMAGAWA - DORI

Though **Dogen-zaka** *(named after a bandit who retired here as a monk) is a nighttime destination, it also has several art galleries.*

→ Strolling Shibuya's busy central shopping street, neon-lit Center Gai

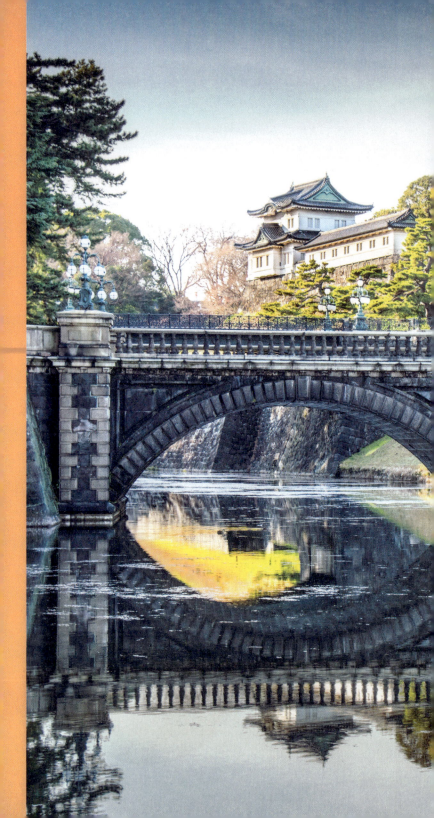

The Imperial Palace, beyond the Nijubashi Bridge

CENTRAL TOKYO

Situated to the north and west of the Sumida River, this area has been at the heart of Tokyo since the shogun Tokugawa Ieyasu built his castle and capital where the Imperial Palace still stands today. When Tokugawa moved his military center here in 1590, it was surrounded by swamp and marshland. Once filled in, the area that became Ginza – "the silver place" – attracted tradesmen and merchants. Destroyed by a series of disasters, including a devastating fire in 872, the Great Kanto Earthquake of 1923, and the Allied bombing in World War II, the area has reinvented itself several times over, but has always remained true to its history as the center of Tokyo.

The area's continuing importance is evident in the Hibiya business district and cosmopolitan Marunouchi, home to the Tokyo International Forum. Ginza and Nihonbashi remain as thriving and prosperous today as they have been since the Edo period (1603–1868), offering a mix of department stores and chic side-street boutiques.

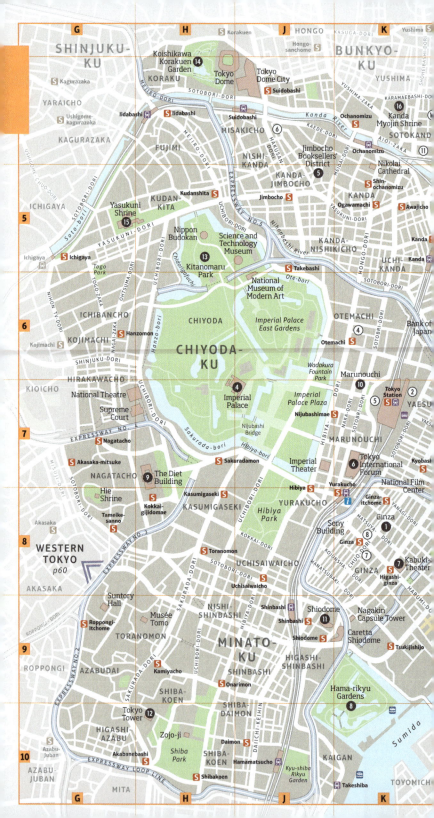

CENTRAL TOKYO

Must Sees
1. Ginza
2. Nihonbashi
3. Akihabara
4. Imperial Palace

Experience More
5. Jimbocho Booksellers' District
6. Tokyo International Forum
7. Kabuki-za Theater
8. Hama-rikyu Gardens
9. The Diet Building
10. Marunouchi
11. Shiodome
12. Tokyo Tower
13. Kitanomaru Park
14. Koishikawa Korakuen Garden
15. Yasukuni Shrine
16. Kanda Myojin Shrine

Eat
1. Takashimaya
2. Rokurinsha
3. Sushi Shin

Stay
4. Aman Tokyo
5. The Tokyo Station Hotel
6. Hotel Niwa Kanda

Shop
7. Ginza Six
8. Ginza Wako
9. Yodobashi Camera
10. Gachapon Kaikan
11. Kotobukiya

❶
GINZA

銀座

◉ K8 Ⓢ Ginza

Tokyo must count as the single greatest city to shop in the world, and Ginza is its Mayfair, Fifth Avenue, and Avenue Montaigne rolled into one. Tiny shops selling traditional crafts mix with trendy galleries and sprawling department stores for an unrivaled shopping experience.

The sophisticated neighborhood of Ginza, with its tree-lined avenues and broad pedestrianized streets, has a more cosmopolitan feel than many other parts of Toyko. The area was destroyed by a devastating fire in 1872 and the newly restored imperial government commissioned Irish architect Thomas Waters to rebuild Ginza in red brick – the height of fashion at the time. The area has never looked back and its leafy streets are now home to some of the most chic boutiques, shopping complexes, and restaurants that the capital has to offer. These include the gargantuan Ginza Six, which focuses on the latest fashion trends, and Ginza Wako, a traditional department store dating from the 1940s. Known as Brand Street, Chuo-dori is home to some of Japan's most prestigious shopping, ranging from department stores such as Matsuya to international fashion boutiques, including Dior, Prada, and Louis Vuitton.

SHOP

Ginza Six
Home to over 240 stores, Ginza Six is the biggest shopping complex in the area. Inside this mammoth store, you'll find big international names, including Céline and Dior.

◉ K8 ⌂ 6-10-1 Ginza
⏱ 10:30am–8:30pm daily ⓦ ginza6.tokyo/welcome-to-gsix

Ginza Wako
With its distinctive clock tower, Wako has been a hard-hitting presence on Ginza's shopping scene for decades. Known for its range of watches, jewelry, chocolate, and porcelain, it's a great place to browse.

◉ K8 ⌂ 4-5-11 Ginza
⏱ 10:30am–7pm daily
ⓦ wako.co.jp

←

Fashion-forward retail concessions in the foyer of Ginza Six

📷 PICTURE PERFECT
Capsule Capture

A short walk from the south end of Chuo-dori is the Nakagin Capsule Tower, a rare example of Japanese Metabolism (p33). Take a picture of this modular building, seemingly built out of washing machines, from across the street.

↑ Walking past the stylish window displays of Chanel on Chuo-dori

Did You Know?

The irregular windows on the Mikimoto Ginza2 building aim to mimic the ocean's surface.

The striking exterior of Mikimoto Ginza2, a jewelry and cosmetics store ↑

A SHORT WALK
GINZA

Distance 1 mile (2 km) **Time** 30 minutes
Nearest subway Yarakucho Station

When Tokugawa Ieyasu moved his military capital to Edo in 1600, Ginza (*p90*) was all swamp and marshland. Once filled in, the area attracted tradesmen and merchants, and the silver mint that provided Ginza's name – "silver place" – was built in 1612. Ever since Thomas Waters rebuilt the area in the 19th century, Ginza has been Japan's epicenter of Western influences and all things modern, and is still one of Tokyo's great commercial centers. Wander Ginza's leafy streets, and take a moment to pop into the many department stores to check out glitzy food halls, where gleaming cabinets display delicious delectables. Some of these mammoth stores even house their own art galleries.

Did You Know?

On Sundays and public holidays, Chuo-Dori Street is closed to traffic.

*The second floor of the **Gallery Center Building** houses exclusive galleries showcasing Japanese and Western art. There is an auction house on the fifth floor.*

Hankyu *department store focuses on fashion, with a mix of Japanese and international labels.*

Yurakucho Station

Hankyu and Seibu

START/FINISH

Sukiyabashi Park

TOKYO EXPRESSWAY

Gallery Center Building

Sony Showroom

SUKIYA-DORI

SOTOBORI-DORI

MIYUKI-DORI

SONY-DORI

Asahi Building

KOJUNSHA-DORI

NAMIKI-DORI

NISHI-GOBANGAI-DORI

The Asahi Building contains a traditional kimono shop, silversmiths, and several boutiques.

Namiki-Dori and **Chuo-Dori** *are lined with boutiques such as Gucci, Dior, Louis Vuitton, and Cartier.*

↑ The facade of the Bulgari store on Chuo-Dori

0 meters   150
0 yards   150

N ↑

This area reflects the Parisian influence on Ginza in the 1930s, with its many French cafés and boutiques.

Locator Map
For more detail see p88

CENTRAL TOKYO

Ginza

Ginza-Itchome S

Printemps

Matsuya Department Store *is another huge store stocking everything from food to bonsai.*

Matsuya Department Store

Mikimoto

Mikimoto Ginza2 *is the district's second branch of this luxury pearl jeweller.*

Wako Department Store

Mitsukoshi Department Store

S **Ginza**

Wako Department Store's *clocktower is a popular symbol of Ginza. The store's window displays are always entertaining.*

San'ai Building

Mitsukoshi Department Store *retains an aura of glamor. Don't miss the sumptuous kimonos.*

Ginza Yon-chome *crossing, one of the busiest in the world, is Ginza's main intersection.*

*Made of glass, the **San'ai Building** is at its best at dusk when the neon signs inside shine through the glass, creating a magical effect.*

→ The striking exterior of Mikimoto Ginza2, illuminated by colored lights

SOTOBORI-DORI
TOKYO EXPRESSWAY
GINZA MARRONNIER-DORI
NAMIKI-DORI
YANAGI-DORI
GINZA RENGA-DORI
GINZA GAS-TOH-DORI
CHUO-DORI
MATSUYA-DORI
NAMIKI-DORI
GINZA RENGA-DORI
GINZA GAS-TOH-DORI
CHUO-DORI
HARUMI-DORI
MATSUYA-DORI
GINZA MIHARA-DORI
CHUO-DORI
HARUMI-DORI
AZUMA-DORI
GINZA MIHARA-KOJI
MIYUKI-DORI

EAT

Takashimaya

The recipe for the sauce used at Takashimaya eel shop has not been altered since the eatery opened in 1875. What's more, this venerable restaurant doesn't just serve up any old eel to its discerning clientele. Only the Kyosui *unagi*, a slow-growing and richer flavored sub-species of the fish, will be found in the kitchen here. A bento option for takeout is available.

🚇 J6 🏠 11-11-15 Nihonbashikobunacho, Chuo 🕐 Sun 🌐 takashimaya.info

¥ ¥ ¥

→

An illuminated street lined with stores in the Nihonbashi district

❷

NIHONBASHI

日本橋

🚇 L6 🚉 & 🚇 Tokyo stn 🚇 Nihonbashi, Mitsukoshimae 🕐 Tokyo Stock Exchange: 9am–4:30pm Mon–Fri 🌐 Tokyo Stock Exchange: jpx.co.jp

The mercantile and entrepreneurial center of Edo and Meiji Tokyo, Nihonbashi has been the city's traditional commercial hub for centuries. It is here, amid the ultramodern streets and buildings, that you will find some of the oldest continuously operating businesses in the world, including dozens of bank headquarters, huge department stores, and smaller traditional stores.

Home to both the Bank of Japan and the Tokyo Stock Exchange, which has an observation deck, Nihonbashi feels as if it is at the center of the city. The district is named after the famous bridge, immortalized in Hokusai's prints of great processions passing over on their way into the shogun's city. The Edo era still feels within touching distance in this densely packed district and, to this day, Nihonbashi remains the center for traditional Japanese small-scale crafts in the city. Kimono-makers, embroiderers, and even toothpick whittlers still sell their wares here. One former kimono shop is Mitsukoshi. Founded in 1673, this labyrinthine complex was Japan's first department store, and serves as a monument to consumption. A newer addition to the neighborhood is the sleek Coredo Muromachi complex. Its three buildings are home to fashion and interior design boutiques, as well as traditional delis, sweet shops, bars, and restaurants. Although trading in the Tokyo Stock Exchange was computerized in 1999, this is still a great place to see the importance of commerce in the capital. The visitors' observation deck overlooks the trading floor.

Did You Know?

In Japan, distances from Tokyo are measured from Nihonbashi bridge.

1 Nihonbashi bridge is decorated with statues of symbolically powerful animals, including lions and dragons.

2 The main hall of Mitsukoshi is crowned with a statue of the Goddess of Sincerity.

3 Although cherry trees can only be found along Edo Sakura-dori, Nihonbashi celebrates the flowering of sakura with many events, including light shows.

③

AKIHABARA

秋葉原

📍L4 🚇&🚉Akihabara

Also known as Akiba, this district is the unofficial capital of some of Japan's most beloved exports: electronics, video games, and anime. The colorful billboards, crowds of eager shoppers, and the mix of multi-level department stores and tiny treasure troves all give Akiba the feeling of a giant geek's playground.

Tokyo's "Electric Town" reinvents itself every 15-20 years. During the postwar years it was a ramshackle market popular for its cheap radio sets, before changing to meet the demand for TVs and washing machines – so much so that as much as 10 per cent of all household appliances sold in Japan were bought here. In the 1980s, the district's major chain stores moved to the suburbs where most families lived, and the focus of Akiba's products moved away from household appliances to the new home computer craze.

As many computer hobbyists were also into video games, manga, and anime, *otaku* (geek) culture began to find its way into

> **Akihabara is a geek capital known around the world, its incredible selection of stores drawing visitors who want to hunt down new, used, and rare goods from the thriving *otaku* industry.**

SHOP

Yodobashi Camera
A vast selection of both *otaku* goods and electronic gadgets.

🏠1-1 Kanda Hanaokacho
🕒9:30am–10pm daily
🌐yodobashi-akiba.com

___

Gachapon Kaikan
Over 400 *gachapon* (capsule machines), with new items coming in every month.

🏠3-15-5 Soto-Kanda
🕒11am–8pm daily (to 7pm Sun)
🌐akibagacha.com

___

Kotobukiya
Showcases what's currently hot in Japan's *otaku* goods.

🏠1-8-8- Soto-Kanda
🕒10am–10pm daily
🌐kotobukiya.co.jp

→

J-Pop and anime ads in the Akihabara district; *(inset)* a shop display of electronic parts

OTAKU CULTURE

Otaku is the Japanese term for people with obsessive interests, particularly in anime and manga – though it's also applied to those passionate about trains, pop stars, and collectibles of various kinds. Although originally a pejorative – like the English word "geek" – an increasing number of people now proudly self-identify as *otaku*. The subculture gained ground in the 1980s, coinciding with the anime boom, as changing social attitudes led many young Japanese people to consider themselves outcasts from traditional society.

Akiba, and by the late 1990s the community had found a home here.

Today, Akihabara is a geek capital known around the world, its incredible selection of stores drawing visitors who want to hunt down new, used, and rare goods from the thriving *otaku* industry. As for the old "electronic heart" of the district, it has survived to this day, with many tiny stores still selling household appliances and gadgets of all kinds.

4

IMPERIAL PALACE

皇居

📍 J7 🏠 1-1 Chiyoda, Chiyoda 🚇 Tokyo 🚇 Nijubashi 🕐 Imperial Palace: Jan 2, Feb 23; East Garden: 9am–4pm Tue–Thu, Sat, Sun (Mar–mid-Apr, Sep & Oct: to 4:30pm; mid-Apr–Aug: to 5pm) 🌐 kunaicho.go.jp

The residence of the emperor of Japan, the Imperial Palace is a modern, working castle at the heart of Tokyo. In a city where everything can feel to be in a permanent state of flux, the palace and its grounds form a green thread of continuity with the capital and Japan's past.

Following the Meiji Restoration in 1868, Japan's imperial family moved from Kyoto to Tokyo. Edo Castle, the former home of the Tokugawa shoguns, was commandeered for the emperor and rechristened the Imperial Palace. None of the main buildings from this period remain today, but the moats, walls, entrance gates, and guardhouses bear testament to this martial past. Most of the palace was destroyed during World War II, but it was rebuilt in the same style. Popular sights include Nijubashi – two bridges that form an entrance to the inner palace grounds – and the East Gardens of the Imperial Palace. The grounds feature Japanese- and Western-style gardens and the foundations of the castle's former keep. Visitors are only able to enter the Imperial Palace on two days each year, but guided tours of the grounds are available throughout the rest of the year at 10am and 1:30pm (registration begins an hour before each tour).

> **In a city where everything can feel to be in a permanent state of flux, the palace and its grounds form a green thread of continuity.**

The imposing Kyuden, the main building of the Imperial Palace ↑

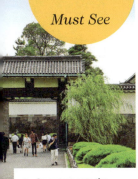

↑ An entrance to the East Gardens of the Imperial Palace

> 💬 **INSIDER TIP**
> ## Poetry at the Palace
>
> A poetry reading called Utakai Hajime is held in the Imperial Palace every New Year's Day. There is a record of the event having taken place as early as 1267. Today it is attended by the emperor and broadcast live on TV, offering glimpses of the palace.

↑ Browsing through stalls selling secondhand books in Jimbocho Booksellers' District

EXPERIENCE MORE

5

Jimbocho Booksellers' District

神保町古本屋街

📍 J5 Ⓢ Jimbocho

Three of the country's great universities – Meiji, Chuo, and Nihon – started out in this area in the 1870s and 1880s, and soon booksellers sprang up selling both new and used books. At one time as many as 50 percent of Japan's publishers were based in this district.

Although only Meiji University and Nihon University are still in the area, dozens of bookshops, including several selling ukiyo-e prints, remain, all clustered around the junction of Yasukuni-dori and Hakusan-dori. For English books on Eastern subjects, try Issei-do or Kitazawa Books; for ukiyo-e prints, visit Ohya Shobo – all are on the south side of Yasukuni-dori, walking away from Hakusan-dori.

The change in the economic status (as well as pastimes and priorities) of Tokyo's university students is evident in Jimbocho Booksellers' District. Shops selling surf- or snowboards are now everywhere, and music shops full of electric guitars seem as numerous as the bookshops.

> ### Did You Know?
> ———
> The Japanese word *tsundoku* means "to buy more books than you can ever read."

The enormous sleek interior of the Tokyo International Forum ↑

7

Kabuki-za Theater
歌舞伎座

K8 4-12-15 Ginza Higashi-Ginza kabuki-za.co.jp

Tokyo's principal theater for Kabuki opened in 1889 during the reign of Emperor Meiji as part of Kabuki's shift from daytime entertainment for the masses in Asakusa to a more high-brow art form.

The theater has seen many incarnations over the years, but still employs traditional Japanese designs. It was almost destroyed by the Allied bombing of 1945, and was rebuilt in 1951, only to be demolished yet again in 2010. The theater reopened in 2013, and enchanting performances, including dance, historical plays and updated Kabuki plays, take place here most evenings.

6

Tokyo International Forum
東京国際フォーラム

K7 3-5-1 Marunouchi & Yurakucho, Tokyo Ginza 7am–11:30pm daily t-i-forum.co.jp

Designed by the renowned American-based architect Rafael Viñoly, and completed in 1996, the International Forum is one of downtown Tokyo's most distinctive buildings. A bustling cultural center, it is made up of two buildings: a curved, glass atrium soaring 200 ft (60 m) into the sky, and a white, cube-like structure housing four halls (with the largest able to seat 5,012). A tree-shaded courtyard separates the two, while glass walkways provide an overhead link. The interior of the huge atrium is filled with natural light and has a ceiling resembling a ship's hull. There are plenty of shops, cafés, and restaurants, as well as conference rooms, all supported by state-of-the-art facilities. High-speed internet access is available in the entrance lobby.

→ The entrance to the much-reconstructed Kabuki-za Theater

↑ The hero of a No performance fighting a masked demon

JAPANESE TRADITIONAL THEATER

Four major types of traditional theater are still performed regularly in Japan: No, Kyogen, Kabuki, and Bunraku. Originating in Shinto rites, No became more ritualistic and ceremonial, before splintering into different forms designed to entertain the masses.

NO

First performed by Kan'ami Kiyotsugu (1333–84), No is a restrained but powerful theatrical form. One or two masked characters appear on the bare stage at a time, and perform slow, choreographed actions *(kata)* to music.

KYOGEN

This form evolved from comic interludes devised as relief from the demanding nature of No. A down-to-earth, colloquial form, its characters highlight human foibles. Rather than masks, the actors wear distinctive yellow *tabi* socks.

KABUKI

If No is stark, Kabuki is flamboyant and colorful. Elaborate make-up replaced No masks, and a curtain allowed set changes. Although Kabuki was founded by a woman, all actors are now male, and female roles are played by highly skilled *onnagata*.

BUNRAKU

Elaborately dressed 4-ft- (1.2-m-) high puppets are manipulated by a puppeteer and his two assistants. *Shamisen* music accompanies the action, and a narrator both tells the story and speaks all the parts.

↑ Elaborately dressed Kabuki performers on stage

↑ A Bunraku puppet striking a ceremonial bell

← A stream running through the charming, tree-filled Hama-rikyu Gardens

pond. Green *matcha* tea and delicious, traditional Japanese sweets are available here.

The Diet Building
国会議事堂

🔲 H7 🅂 Kokkai-Gijidomae, Nagatacho 🕒 8am–5pm Mon–Fri (by reservation) 🆆 sangiin.go.jp

Completed in 1936, the Diet Building houses the legislature of the Japanese government, originally established as the Imperial Diet in the Meiji era. Tours (in Japanese only) cover the well-worn inside, including the Diet chamber, where you can see the deliberations of Diet members, and the extravagantly decorated rooms formerly used by the emperor for official functions.

Nearby, you'll find Central Tokyo's only Western-style park, Hibiya Park. Its location, close to the political centers

Hama-rikyu Gardens
浜離宮庭園

🔲 K9 📞 (03) 3541-0200 Ⓢ Shinbashi 🅂 Shiodome 🕒 9am–5pm daily

Situated where the Sumida River empties into Tokyo Bay, this 62-acre (25-hectare) garden dotted with colorful and fragrant plants like camellia and azalea was built in 1654 as a retreat for the shogun's family, who

INSIDER TIP
All Aboard!

A cruise on the Sumida River from Hama-rikyu Gardens to Asakusa in Northern Tokyo offers a little-seen view of the city. In spaceship-like or retro-style boats, you'll pass under bridges, take in the city's soaring skyscrapers, and see people relaxing in the parks by the water. Near Asakusa there are long, low boats that take out groups for lantern-lit evening cruises *(www.suijo bus.co.jp).*

also hunted duck here. The garden has had an illustrious history. The US president Ulysses S. Grant stayed in a villa in the gardens during his visit in 1879 and sipped green tea in Nakajima teahouse.

The garden grounds surrounding the duck ponds are still a pleasant and uncrowded place to stroll and unwind, although all of the original teahouses and villas, trees, and vegetation burned down after a devastating bombing raid on November 29, 1944. But Nakajima teahouse has been faithfully rebuilt, appearing to float over the large

→ The grand entrance to Tokyo Station, in the Marunouchi district

of Kasumigaseki and the Diet Building, makes it a favorite place for protests, especially on May Day. The large bandstand is used for concerts.

 Marunouchi
丸の内

K7 & Tokyo

During the Edo era, this district earned the name "Gambler's Meadow" as its isolation made it an ideal place to gamble secretly. The area was used by the army in the Meiji period before selling it to Mitsubishi in 1890. The arrival of the railroad increased the desirability of this barren wasteland as a business site, and after the 1923 earthquake, many other firms moved here.

Tokyo Station, designed by Kingo Tatsuno and completed in 1914, is supposedly based on the design of Amsterdam's Centraal Station. Its dome was damaged in the 1945 air raids and subsequently replaced by the polyhedron there today. The original reliefs adorning the domes above the North and South exits are worth a look. Opposite the station's south gate is the shopping mall KITTE, with the **Tokyo City-i** information center on the first floor. The English-speaking staff here, including Pepper the robot, offer advice and help to visitors.

For those interested in traditional Japanese arts and crafts, the **Idemitsu Museum of Arts** showcases the vast art collection of Sazo Idemitsu, the founder of one of Japan's largest oil companies. The regularly changing exhibits display astonishing examples of Japanese calligraphy and paintings, as well as Japanese and Chinese ceramics.

Tokyo City-i
2-7-2 Marunouchi, Chiyoda 8am–8pm daily en.tokyocity-ijp

Idemitsu Museum of Arts
 Teigeki Building, 3-1-1 Marunouchi 10am–4pm Tue–Thu, Sat & Sun, 10am–7pm Fri idemitsu-museum.or.jp

STAY

Aman Tokyo
A glamorous high-rise hotel, with a hot tub in each room.
K6 1-5-6 Otemachi, Chiyoda aman.com

The Tokyo Station Hotel
Next to Tokyo Station, this luxury hotel is an oasis of calm and peace.
K7 1-9-1 Marunouchi, Chiyoda thetokyostation hotel.jp/en

¥¥¥

Hotel Niwa Kanda
This hotel blends the look of a traditional Japanese inn with contemporary touches.
J4 1-1-16 Kanda Misakicho, Chiyoda hotelniwa.jp

¥¥¥

Nakajima teahouse in the Hama-rikyu Gardens

11

Shiodome
汐留

Q J9 **R** Shimbashi
S Shiodome

In the late 1980s, waterfront development became Tokyo's new frontier. The Shiodome City Center complex, which was opened in 2003, is one of the more successful of these waterfront developments. Within this grove of ultra-modern skyscrapers are the impressive, triangular Shiodome Media Tower, headquarters of Kyodo News and home to Park Hotel Tokyo; and Acty Shiodome, one of the tallest residential buildings in Japan. It is made up of 56 stories, and has indoor malls and an outdoor piazza, providing exciting places to dine or shop. Nearby is ADMT, the Advertising Museum of Tokyo, located in the basement of the Caretta Shiodome, which has the offices of the world's largest advertising agency – Dentsu.

For further exploration of the Tokyo Bay area, take the Yurikamome Line from Shiodome Station toward Rainbow Bridge, and enjoy great views of the Sumida River and the futuristic island of Odaiba (p149).

12

Tokyo Tower
東京タワー

Q H10 **S** Akabanebashi
◷ 9am-11pm daily
w tokyotower.co.jp

The striking Tokyo Tower was erected partly as a symbol of Japan's postwar boom, as well as to act as the sole broadcasting tower for the whole Kanto region. Two observation

→

The soaring Tokyo Tower, inspired by Paris's Eiffel Tower, seen at sunset

Did You Know?

Zojo-ji temple in Shiba Park is home to a fifth-century grave mound, untouched by time.

decks – the Main Deck at 492 ft (150 m) and the Top Deck at 820 ft (250 m) – offer spectacular views of Tokyo Bay, the nearby districts of Shimbashi and Ginza, and Mount Fuji on a clear day.

As a lofty symbol of the city, it may have been usurped by Tokyo SkyTree (p127), but Tokyo Tower is still worth a visit for the views, as well as for the many amusements, cafés, and shops in "Foot Town", the building at the tower's base.

To the east of Tokyo Tower extends Shiba Park, at the center of which lies **Zojo-ji**, the Tokugawa family temple, It was founded in 1393, and Ieyasu moved it here in 1598 to protect his new capital. The present-day temple dates from 1974; nearby are the re-built Daimon (big gate) and

the Sanmon (great gate), built in 1622, and the oldest wooden structure in Tokyo.

Zojo-ji
w zojoji.or.jp

13

Kitanomaru Park
北の丸公園

Q H5 **S** Kudanshita, Takebashi

Lying to the north of the Imperial Palace, Kitanomaru Park is reached through the massive Tayasumon gate. A former ground for the Imperial Palace Guard, the area became a park in 1969. Before entering, walk past Tayasumon gate on the left to reach Chidorigafuchi (the west moat), one of Tokyo's most beautiful cherry-blossom viewing spots. Rowboats can be rented here.

Within Kitanomaru's grounds is the indoor arena, Nippon Budokan. Built for the 1964 Olympics martial arts competition, it is now used mostly for rock concerts. Farther on is the **Science and Technology Museum**. The fun interactive exhibits include

People rowing on a lake and *(inset)* strolling in Kitanomaru Park during cherry-blossom season

virtual car, truck, and bike rides and electricity demonstrations (explanations are in Japanese).

Five minutes' walk beyond is the **National Museum of Modern Art**. The permanent collection comprises Japanese works from the 1868 Meiji Restoration to the present day; visiting exhibits are often excellent. Nearby is the National Museum of Modern Art's **Crafts Gallery**. Inside this 1910 Neo-Gothic brick building is an exquisite collection of modern workings of traditional Japanese crafts – pottery, lacquerware, and damascene (inlaid etched metal artifacts). Some pieces are also for sale.

Science and Technology Museum

 2-1 Kitanomaru Koen, Chiyoda ⏰ 9:30am–4:50pm Thu–Tue 🌐 jsf.or.jp

National Museum of Modern Art

3-1 Kitanomaru Koen, Chiyoda ⏰ 10am–5pm Tue–Sun (to 8pm Fri & Sat) 🌐 momat.go.jp/english/am

Crafts Gallery

1-1 Kitanomaru Koen, Chiyoda ⏰ 10am–5pm Tue–Sun 🌐 momat.go.jp/english/am

14

Koishikawa Korakuen Garden
小石川後楽園

📍 H4 🏠 1-6-6 Koraku, Bunkyo 📞 (03) 3811-3015 🚇 Korakuen ⏰ 9am–5pm daily

This is one of Tokyo's most delightful traditional stroll gardens. Construction started in 1629 and finished 30 years later. Exiled Chinese scholar Zhu Shunsui helped design the garden, including the Engetsukyo (full-moon) bridge, a stone arch with a reflection resembling a full moon. Tsutenkyo bridge is striking for the contrast between its vermilion color and the surrounding deep-green forest. The garden represents larger landscapes in miniature, including Rozan, a famous Chinese mountain, and Kyoto's Oikawa River. In the middle of the large pond is Horai Island, a beautiful composition of stone and pine trees.

EAT

Rokurinsha

You may have to wait in line to get into this popular ramen spot. Try the *tsuke-men*, where noodles are served separately and dunked into a thickened broth.

📍 K7 🏠 1 Chome-9-1, Marunouchi, Chiyoda 📞 (03) 3286-0166

Sushi Shin

Located in the Mandarin Oriental, this Michelin-starred sushi restaurant offers a stunning view of the Tokyo skyline.

📍 L6 🏠 -1-1 Nihonbashi Muromachi, Chuo 📞 (03) 3270-8634

15 Yasukuni Shrine
靖国神社

📍 G5 🏠 3-1-1 Kudankita, Chiyoda 🚇 Kudanshita
🕐 6am-6pm daily (Nov-Feb: to 5pm) 🌐 yasukuni.or.jp

The 2.5 million Japanese soldiers and civilians who have died in war since the Meiji Restoration in 1868 are enshrined at Yasukuni Jinja (Shrine of Peace for the Nation). It is a sobering place to visit.

Until the end of World War II, Shinto was the official state religion, and the ashes of all who died in war were brought here regardless of the families' wishes. Controversially, the planners and leaders of Japan during World War II and the colonization of China and Korea are also enshrined here, including wartime prime minister Hideki Tojo.

Beside the shrine is the **Yushukan**, a museum dedicated to the war dead. Many exhibits put a human face to Japan at war; under a photo of a smiling young officer is a copy of his last letter home, and there are mementos of a nurse who died from overwork. Still, romanticized paintings of Japanese soldiers in Manchuria and displays of guns, planes, and even a locomotive from the Thai–Burma Railway may be disturbing to some.

Yushukan
 🕐 9am-4:30pm daily

---

16 Kanda Myojin Shrine
神田明神

📍 K4 📞 (03) 3254-0753
🚃 & 🚇 Ochanomizu
🕐 24 hours daily

Myojin is over 1,200 years old, although the present structure is a reproduction built after the 1923 earthquake. The gate's guardian figures are two archers: Udaijin on the right and Sadaijin on the left. Just inside the compound on the left is a big stone statue of Daikoku, one of the *shichi-fuku-jin* (seven lucky gods). Here, as always, he is sitting on top of two huge rice bales.

The vermilion shrine itself and its beautiful interior, all lacquer and gold and ornate Chinese-style decoration, are very impressive. Early morning is the best time to glimpse the Shinto priests performing rituals. The Kanda Matsuri, celebrated in May, is one of the greatest and grandest of Tokyo's festivals – come early and be prepared for crowds.

Behind the main shrine is a **museum** containing relics from the long history of Myojin.

Museum
 🕐 9am-4pm daily

THE YASUKUNI CONTROVERSY

Since 1869, Yasukuni has honored the souls of those who have died in the service of Japan. The shrine is a place of remembrance for millions of Japanese who lost relatives fighting for their country. Among these, however, are about 1,000 war criminals from World War II. The perception that these souls are being honored has made Yasukuni a site of enormous controversy among Japan's neighbors who suffered greatly during the war as a result of their actions.

↑ The distinctive vermilion exterior of Kanda Myojin Shrine

↑ The brightly colored main hall of Kanda Myojin, a shrine in Tokyo's Chiyoda district

SHINTO

Japan's oldest religion, Shinto's core concept is that deities, *kami*, preside over all things in nature, be they living, dead, or inanimate. Today, there are few pure Shintoists, but *jinja* (shrines) still line waysides and Shinto rituals are observed alongside Buddhist practices.

SACRED GATES

The approach to the *jinja* transports worshippers from the secular to the sacred world. Vermilion torii often line the path, symbolizing gateways, and red-bibbed stone foxes stand guard at Inari Shrines. Inside the shrine's main complex, *shimenawa*, a rope made of twisted rice straw, hangs over entrances to ward off evil and sickness.

HAIDEN AND HONDEN

At the *haiden*, or hall of worship, devotees pull on a bell rope, toss money into a box, clap three times to summon the resident *kami*, then stand in silent prayer for a few moments. The *kami* is believed to live in the shrine's *honden* (main sanctuary), but usually only the head priests are permitted to enter this hallowed space.

KANNUSHI

The Shinto priesthood *(kannushi)* tended to be passed down through families, and some of these dynasties *(shake)* are still connected with certain shrines. Usually dressed in white and orange robes, the *kannushi* perform purification ceremonies and other rituals.

CHARMS AND VOTIVE TABLETS

Good-luck charms, called *omamori*, are sold at shrines across Japan. Common themes relate to fertility, luck in examinations, general health, or safety while driving. The charm itself might be written on a piece of paper or thin wooden board and tucked into a cloth bag, which can be worn next to the body or placed somewhere relevant. Do not open the bag to read the charm or it will not work! Prayers or wishes can also be written on *ema* boards *(above)* and hung at the shrine.

→ A cloth bag containing a paper *omamori*

NORTHERN TOKYO

The northern districts of Ueno and Asakusa contain what remains of Tokyo's old Shitamachi (low city). Once the heart and soul of culture in Edo, Shitamachi became the subject of countless ukiyo-e wood-block prints. Merchants and artisans thrived here, as did Kabuki theater. As a consequence of this liberal atmosphere, the Yoshiwara red-light district moved near Asakusa in the 17th century after the Great Fire of Meireki destroyed nearly 70 per cent of the city in 1657. By 1893 there were over 9,000 women living and working in this raucous area.

Shops, restaurants, and museums in Asakusa tend to revolve around traditional culture, thanks to the influence of the district's most important site, the bustling Senso-ji temple, which keeps history at the forefront of the local community. Ueno, meanwhile, is known for its vast and beautiful park. In the late 19th century, Dr Anthonius Baudin, a Dutch military doctor, observed the area's natural beauty and successfully petitioned for the land to be turned into one of Japan's first public parks, rather than the proposed army hospital and cemetery. The park became a haven for art and thought, hosting the first and second National Industrial Exhibitions in 1887 and 1881 respectively, and becoming home to the Tokyo National Museum in 1882.

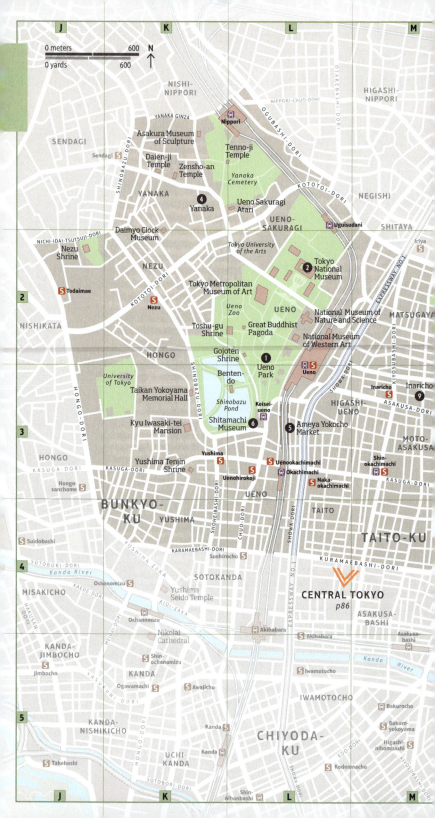

NORTHERN TOKYO

Must Sees
1. Ueno Park
2. Tokyo National Museum
3. Senso-ji

Experience More
4. Yanaka
5. Ameya Yokocho Market
6. Shitamachi Museum
7. Tokyo Skytree
8. Drum Museum
9. Inaricho and Kappabashi-dori
10. Asakusa

Eat
1. Nakasei
2. Izakaya Koji
3. Ocomo
4. Ninja Cafe & Bar

Shop
5. Kamata

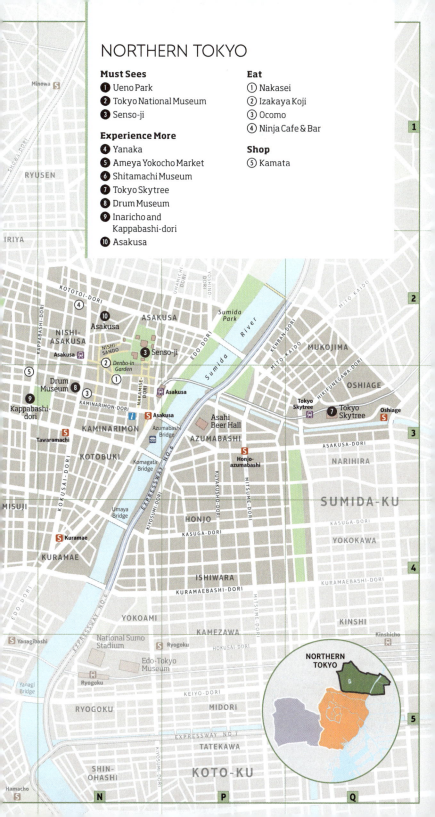

1

UENO PARK

上野公園

📍 L2 🏠 5-20 Uenokoen, Taito 🚃 Uguisudani
🚃 & 🚇 Ueno 🕐 Times vary, check websites for details
🌐 Ueno Zoo: tokyo-zoo.net; Tokyo Metropolitan Art
Museum: tobikan.jp; National Museum of Nature and
Science: kahaku.go.jp; National Museum of Western
Art: nmwa.go.jp

Erupting in a riot of pink cherry blossoms every
spring, it is little wonder that Ueno Park, one of
Tokyo's most beautiful green spaces, has figured
in so many woodblock prints and stories.

Ieyasu, the first Tokugawa shogun, built the
Kan'ei-ji temple and subtemples in Ueno in the
1600s to negate evil spirits from the northeast.
Judging by how long the Tokugawas lasted, it
was a wise move, and parts of the temple still
stand. In 1873, five years after the Battle of
Ueno, when the last supporters of the shogun
were crushed by imperial forces, the government designated Ueno a public park. It has been
a popular spot ever since for Tokyo locals to
relax. As well as its tranquil tree-lined paths,
Shinobazu Pond (actually three ponds) is an
annual stop for thousands of migrating birds.
Ueno Park is home to the Tosho-gu Shrine and
Japan's oldest zoo, as well as a whole host of
museums. There's the Tokyo Metropolitan Art
Museum, displaying contemporary Japanese
art, the extensive National Museum of Western
Art, and the National Museum of Nature and
Science, with its jaw-dropping dinosaur
skeletons. Topping them all is the vast Tokyo
National Museum (p118).

> 💬 INSIDER TIP
> **Sakura Spotting**
>
> Some 800 sakura
> (cherry) trees grow in
> Ueno Park. Over a brief
> period every spring,
> more than 2 million
> people visit the park
> for *hanami* (cherry-
> blossom-viewing)
> picnics. To find out the
> best time to sit beneath
> the blossoming trees
> for your own *hanami*
> picnic, check the sakura
> forecast online *(sakura.
> weathermap.jp)*.

> **Did You Know?**
> ———
> Before *hanami, umemi*
> (plum-viewing) was
> enjoyed during the
> Nara period.

People enjoying *hanami* ↑
picnics under the cherry
blossoms in Ueno Park

← Skeletons on display in the dinosaur gallery of the family-friendly National Museum of Nature and Science

→ One of the ornate Edo-era halls that make up the Tosho-gu Shrine, where Ieyasu was first enshrined

→ Statue of Saigo Takamori, the leader of the victorious Meiji forces, located near the site of the old Kan'ei-ji temple

THE FOUR SEASONS

Japan's four distinct seasons are a source of national pride, each one bursting with its own beauty and traditions. Even in ultra-modern Tokyo, the heart of cultural life still beats to the rhythm of the four seasons, which dictate the cuisine, fashion, and social events throughout the year. Japan's spring-time sakura blossoms are well known around the world, but there are countless highlights to discover in summer, fall, and winter, as each season changes the appearance and atmosphere of Tokyo, and the landscape of the rural areas outside the city.

The Seasons

Spring

By the time spring is officially declared on Shunbun no Hi (Vernal Equinox Day) on March 21, the weather is mostly warm and sunny in Tokyo. From late March to early April, the brief but beautiful sakura season brings with it the bittersweet feeling known as *mono no aware*: awareness of the impermanent. Later in April, the vibrantly pink azaleas bloom, celebrated with a festival at Nezu Shrine *(p132)*.

Summer

The tinkling of *furin* (cooling wind chimes), the relentless humming of cicada, sighs of "*Atsui!*" ("It's hot!") - these are the sounds of summer in Japan. This is the best season to explore outside the city, so head to the seaside town of Kamakura *(p160)*, or visit the Fuji Five Lakes *(p168)* to enjoy the cooler mountain air. This is also the time to climb Mount Fuji during its short open season (July-September).

↑ Kamakura's lovely summer hydrangeas

Japan's spring-time sakura blossoms are well known around the world, but there are also countless highlights to discover in summer, fall, and winter.

Fall

In a similar way to the sakura obsession of spring, *koyo* (red leaves) come to the fore in fall. Bursts of red and gold brighten the streets of Tokyo, but many people make a trip to the mountains just to enjoy the seasonal colors. Nikko *(p172)* is one of the best options, as the beautiful scenery is accompanied by the Shuki Taisai Grand Autumn Festival in mid-October, which includes impressive displays of *yabusame* (horseback archery).

Winter

Winter is a time of traditions both old and modern. Christmas has been adopted as an annual date night, whereas New Year's is a time for friends, family, and watching TV. Coming of Age Day in January is an important milestone for young people, who dress in traditional clothes for festive ceremonies. The colder months are the time to head out to rural areas such as Hakone *(p178)* to soak in a warm *rotenburo* (outdoor hot spring).

↑ Snow falling in Rikugi-en Garden in Tokyo

Locator Map
For more detail see p112

EAT

Tonkatsu Yamabe

Instead of having lunch at one of the museum's pricey restaurants, head here for tasty *tonkatsu* (breaded pork).

📍 J3 🏠 4-5-1 Ueno
📞 (03) 5817-7045

¥ ¥ ¥

1 The Western-style works of Kuroda Seiki, including *Lakeside* (1897), are displayed in the Kuroda Memorial Hall.

2 Visitors examining exhibits on the first floor of the Honkan building, which houses traditional crafts including pottery and metalwork.

3 The Gallery of Horyu-ji Treasures displays a collection of items from the temple, including rare statues dating from the 7th to 8th centuries.

Must See

↑ The exterior of Honkan, the main building of the Tokyo National Museum

② 🗡 🎎 🍴 🖼 🛍

TOKYO NATIONAL MUSEUM

東京国立博物館

📍 L2 🏠 13-Ueno Park, Taito 🚇 & Ⓢ Ueno 🕐 9:30am–5pm Tue–Sun 🌐 tnm.jp

Seven buildings in the northeast corner of Ueno Park make up one of Tokyo's finest museum complexes. Displaying artifacts from 10,000 BC up to modern 20th century art, it provides an intriguing and thorough insight into Japan's history and culture.

More than 110,000 items make up the Tokyo National Museum's collection – the best assembly of Japanese art in the world – and the displays change frequently, with about 4,000 of these exhibits on public view at any one time. The museum also stages temporary exhibitions, covering art from around the world. If you only have a couple of hours to spare, stick to the second floor of the Honkan gallery. With audio guides, tours, and good signage in English, it's a great introduction to Japanese heritage. Those with the luxury of more time can explore the museum's other buildings, admiring ancient statues, Chinese ceramics and Impressionist paintings at their leisure.

Did You Know?

The Tokyo National Museum is the oldest museum in Japan.

A wooden statue of a ↑
Shinto deity on display
in the Honkan gallery

Exploring the Galleries

The Honkan is the museum's main building, housing Japanese art from ancient finds to modern masters. To its east is the Toyokan, housing non-Japanese Eastern art. The 1909 Beaux-Arts Hyokeikan is usually closed to the public and opens only for special exhibitions. Behind it is the Gallery of Horyu-ji Treasures, containing stunning objects from Horyu-ji temple, near Nara, and the Heiseikan, which hosts exhibitions of archaeology. Access to all of the museum's buildings is included in the cost of one admission ticket, so set out to explore as much of this expansive museum as possible.

Did You Know?

Ukiyo-e translates as "pictures of the floating world."

A folding screen by ↑
Okamoto Shuki on display
in the Honkan gallery

Museum Galleries

Honkan

▷ Spanning two floors, this gallery is arranged chronologically to show the development of Japanese art, from Jomon-era (from 10,000 BC) clay figures to 19th-century ukiyo-e woodblock prints showing everything from landscapes to scenes from pleasure houses *(right)*. In between is everything from calligraphy and tea utensils to armor, as well as textiles used in No and Kabuki. The first floor is themed, with stunning exhibits of sculpture, lacquer-ware, swords, and Western-influenced modern art. The gallery is best navigated by working your way counterclockwise.

Toyokan

Toyokan displays an excellent and eclectic collection of Asian art that ranges from textiles to ceramics. Many of the exhibits are from China and Korea - a result of their long ties with Japan. In the basement is a collection of ceramics, sculptures and archaeological finds from Southeast Asia. On the first floor, you'll find beautiful Buddhist statues, while the second floor houses artifacts from India, Egypt, and the Middle East. A collection of Chinese art spans the third and fourth floors, and the final floor is dedicated to the history of Korea.

Heiseikan

Built in 1993 to commemorate the Crown Prince's wedding - its name translates as "to express congratulations" - the Heiseikan houses major temporary exhibitions and a superb collection of Japanese archaeological artifacts, with items from 10,000 BC onward. The highlight of this collection is undoubtedly the Haniwa figures. Literally meaning "clay ring," Haniwa is used to describe earthenware sculptures that were made for 4th- to 7th-century tombs and were thought to protect the dead. The gallery also houses Jomon-period (14,500-300 BC) finds, including dogu, ceramic figures with bulging eyes.

Gallery of Horyu-Ji Treasures

◁ When the estates of Horyu-ji temple near Nara were damaged during the Meiji reforms, the impoverished temple gave a number of its treasures to the imperial family in exchange for money to finance its repairs. Over 300 of those priceless treasures *(left)*, including rare and early Buddhist statues, masks used for Gigaku dances, and beautifully painted screens, are housed in this modern gallery, designed by Yoshio Taniguchi.

Kuroda Memorial Hall

Dedicated to Kuroda Seiki (1866-1924), this building displays the Western-style artist's oil paintings, sketches and other works. There is also a collection of letters from the painter, giving a greater insight into Kuroda's life and times.

3 🏛

SENSO-JI
浅草寺

📍N2 🏠2 Chome-3-1 Asakusa, Taito 🚆Tobu-Asakusa Ⓐ&Ⓢ Asakusa
🕐Main Hall: 6am-5pm daily (Oct-Mar: 6:30am-5pm); Nakamise-dori: 9:30am-7pm daily (individual store hours vary)

Popularly known as Asakusa Kannon, this is Tokyo's most sacred and spectacular Buddhist temple, as well as the city's oldest. Although the buildings are impressive, it is the people following their daily rituals that make this place so special.

In AD 628, two fishermen pulled a small gold statue of Kannon, the Buddhist goddess of mercy, from the Sumida River. First, their master built a shrine to Kannon, then, in 645, the holy man Shokai built a temple to her. Senso-ji's fame, wealth, and size grew until Tokugawa Ieyasu (p54) bestowed upon it a large stipend of land. When the Yoshiwara pleasure quarter moved nearby in 1657, the temple became even more popular. Senso-ji survived the Great Kanto Earthquake of 1923, but not Allied bombing during World War II. Its main buildings are therefore relatively new, but follow the original Edo-era layout. Today, incense still wafts through the air, and people teem along the wide shopping avenue Nakamise-dori leading to the temple.

The Garden

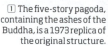

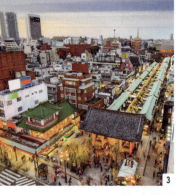

1 The five-story pagoda, containing the ashes of the Buddha, is a 1973 replica of the original structure.

2 Built of reinforced concrete in 1964, the two-story Hozomon Gate has a treasure house upstairs holding a number of 14th-century Chinese sutras.

3 The shops lining the expansive Nakamise-dori sell souvenirs including fans, dolls, and kimonos.

The Kaminarimon Gate, or "Thunder Gate," is topped by guardian statues of Fujin (right) and Raijin (left), which have elderly heads and young bodies.

Awashima-do Hall

Yogodo Hall houses eight Buddha statues.

Five-Story Pagoda

The main hall, which is decorated with paintings, houses the original Kannon image in a gold-plated shrine.

Asakusa Shrine, built in 1649, is dedicated to the fishermen who found the Kannon statue.

Niten-mon gate was built in 1618.

Incense Burner

Hozo-mon Gate

The bell in the Benten-yama Shoro belfry used to ring on the hour in Edo.

Nakamise-dori is a treasure trove of souvenirs.

← Senso-ji's vast complex, reached by the long Nakamise-dori

↑ Looking down Nakamise-dori towards the Hozo-mon Gate

INSIDER TIP
Asakusa District

Senso-ji sits at the heart of Asakusa *(p129)*, where the atmosphere of postwar Tokyo survives. After visiting the temple, explore the backstreets of this old-fashioned neighborhood to find traditional eateries and shops.

The giant Hozo-mon Gate at the entrance of Senso-ji temple

Unassuming entrance to the Asakura Museum of Sculpture

EXPERIENCE MORE

 4

Yanaka
谷中

H2 **Nippori**

This quiet area is rewarding to wander through because it survived the 1923 earthquake and bombing during World War II. It preserves the feeling of old Tokyo, with tightly packed houses in narrow alleys, and traditional food stalls selling old-fashioned candy. Yanaka Cemetery is a must-see in cherry-blossom season. Inside is Tenno-ji, a temple with a large bronze Buddha dating from 1690. To the west of Tenno-ji is the **Asakura Museum of Sculpture**, home of sculptor Fumio Asakura (1883–1964). On the second floor is a delightful room full of statues of one of his favorite subjects – cats – but the garden is the real highlight, with its traditional composition of water and stone. To the north, Yanaka Ginza, the area's shopping street, has traditional stores and family-run places to eat.

JAPANESE FUNERAL CUSTOMS

When a Japanese person dies, the body is brought back home to spend one final night on his or her own futon. The next morning, it is taken to the service at a site such as Yanaka Cemetery. At the wake, guests offer gifts of money and, after the cremation, the family use a special pair of chopsticks to pick the bones out and transfer them to an urn. Remembrance ceremonies are held in the following years on the anniversary of the death.

SHOP

Kamata
Made in Kappabashi, Kamata's famous knives are crafted from the same metal and to the same principles as samurai swords. A must for all keen chefs.

K3 **2-12-6 Matsugaya, Taito** **kap-kam.com**

The understated **Daimyo Clock Museum** has 100 Edo-era clocks lovingly presented.

Asakura Museum of Sculpture

7-18-10 Yanaka, Taito **(03) 3821-4549** **9:30am–4:30pm Tue–Wed & Fri–Sun**

Daimyo Clock Museum

2-1-27 Yanaka, Taito **(03) 3821-6913** **Jan 15–Jun 30 & Oct 1–Dec 24: 10am–4pm Tue–Sun**

 5

Ameya Yokocho Market
アメヤ横丁

L3 **&Ueno** **Okachimachi** **Ueno-Okachimachi**

A fun and busy market street, Ameya Yokocho – commonly known as Ameyoko – sells anything from clothes and bags to fresh fish and spices – and usually at a discount. During the Edo era, the market was full of candy stores (ame-ya). After World War II, black-market goods – such as liquor, cigarettes, and nylons started appearing here, and ame acquired its second meaning as an abbreviation for American. An area of tiny shops packed under the elevated train tracks, Ameyoko is no longer a black market, but still the place for bargain foreign brands. Clothes and accessories are concentrated under the tracks, while foods line the street that follows the tracks.

6

Shitamachi Museum
下町風俗資料館

Q J3 **A** 2-1 Ueno-koen, Taito **C** (03) 3823-7451 **R** Keisei-Ueno, Ueno **S** Ueno **O** 9:30am-4:30pm Tue-Sun

This museum is dedicated to preserving the spirit and artifacts of Shitamachi Tokyo, the area around the Sumida River that was historically home to the lower classes. The 50,000 exhibits include recreations of Edo-era shops, traditional toys, tools, and photographs, all donated by Shitamachi residents.

7

Tokyo Skytree
東京スカイツリー

Q Q3 **A** 1-1-2 Oshiage, Sumida **R** & **S** Tokyo Skytree, Oshiage **O** 8am-9:45pm daily **W** tokyo-skytree.jp

At 2,080 ft (634 m), this is the tallest building in Japan. While its main function is broadcasting, the Skytree also hosts a large mall, aquarium, planetarium, and restaurants. The Tembo Deck, at 1,150 ft (350 m) above ground level, offers 360-degree views. Another viewing deck, Tembo Galleria, is the highest observation deck in Japan at 1,475 ft (450 m). On a clear day you can see as far as Mount Fuji.

→

Slender silhouette of the Tokyo Skytree, towering above the city's skyline

↑ The Drum Museum, with its collection of 800 drums from Japan and around the world

8

Drum Museum
太鼓館

📍 N3 Ⓢ Tawaramachi
📞 (03) 3842-5622 🕙 10am–5pm Wed–Sun

Over 800 drums from across Japan and the world are on display at this museum. None of the text describing the instruments is in English, but a world map on the wall shows the provenance of each drum, including *diembe* drums from Mali, *cuicas* from Brazil, chimes of Chinese origin, and wedding drums from Benin.

All the drums marked with a quaver can be played. However, parents and guardians should still keep an eye on younger visitors, as a blue dot warns that a more delicate handling is required, and a red dot signifies "do not touch." The museum's gift shop sells a good selection of local crafts and even a few drums.

2 million

The number of visitors who often attend Asakusa's Sanja Matsuri festival.

9

Inaricho and Kappabashi-dori
稲荷町とかっぱ橋通り

📍 M3 Ⓢ Inaricho, Tawaramachi

Inaricho District is the Tokyo headquarters for wholesale religious goods. Small wooden boxes to hold Buddhas and family photos, paper lanterns, bouquets of brass flowers *(jouka)*, Shinto household shrines, and even prayer beads can be found here.

The district of Kappabashi-dori is named after the mythical water imps *(kappa)*, who supposedly helped build a bridge *(bashi)* here. The 2019 anime *Sarazanmai* featured many locations from the area, including the district's *kappa* statue (2-Chome-25-9 Matsugaya, Taito), which is a great place for fans to get in some *butaitanbou* (p42). Despite the mythological

> **The district of Kappabashi-dori is named after the mythical water imps (*kappa*), who supposedly helped build a bridge (*bashi*) here.**

name, the district is actually Tokyo's center for kitchenware and the source of the plastic food displayed in restaurant windows. Although the "food" is for sale, prices are much higher than for the real thing.

 10

Asakusa
浅草

⦿ N2 🚇 & Ⓢ Asakusa

Asakusa is one of the most popular sightseeing districts in Tokyo. During the Edo era (1603–1868), this bustling entertainment neighborhood was the home of Kabuki theater and host to an enormous red-light district, both of which became key subjects of the ukiyo-e art movement (p150).

Despite heavy bombing during World War II and modern developments along the Sumida river next door, Asakusa's streets are still characterized by tightly packed alleyways and lanes filled with an assortment of traditional restaurants and shops. The Nishi Sando covered street, in particular, evokes Asakusa's Edo era heyday, with its wooden floors, vermilion columns and balconies, and old-fashioned decor.

EAT

Nakasei
This venerable tempura restaurant has been going strong for almost 150 years. Try their legendary *kakiagedon*, a bowl of rice topped with crispy deep-fried prawn and clam.

⦿ N3 🏠 1-39-13 Asakusa, Taito Ⓒ (03) 3841-4015

Izakaya Koji
One of the best taverns on Asakusa's bar-lined "Hoppy Street". In traditional *izakaya* style, patrons order lots of small dishes while drinking; the beef stew is the house specialty.

⦿ N2 🏠 2-3-19 Asakusa, Taito Ⓒ (03) 3844-0612

Ocomo
Enjoy one of Osaka's regional specialties without leaving Tokyo. Here *okonomiyaki* (savory pancake) is cooked on a hot plate right at your table.

⦿ N3 🏠 1-10-5 Asakusa, Taito Ⓦ ocomo.jp

Ⓢ Ⓢ Ⓢ

Ninja Cafe & Bar
A café with much more than just a themed menu. Come here for family-friendly ninja training, photos with entertaining staff, and walks around Asakusa in full ninja gear.

⦿ N2 🏠 3-27-14 Nishi-asakusa, Taito Ⓦ mordern-izakaya-restaurants-133.business.site

↑ Asahi Beer Hall with the Asahi Flame, by Philippe Starck, near Asakusa's Azuma-Bashi bridge

A LONG WALK

FROM THE HIGH CITY TO THE LOW CITY

Distance 2 miles (3.5 km) **Walking time** 50 minutes
Terrain An easy route along city streets **Nearest station** Yushima Metro Station

This walk follows the slopes of Tokyo's High City (known as Yamanote) down to the flat, river lands of the Low City (Shitamachi). While the names are unofficial and the boundaries have never been formally defined, the split between the High City and Low City has existed in Tokyo culture since the Tokugawa Shogunate was established here in 1603. The Yamanote area was traditionally the home of military leaders and aristocrats, while the Shitamachi districts were the home of the working class. This walk gives you a chance to visit both sides of Tokyo, and the Shitamachi districts in particular are now some of the best places to find neighborhoods with a traditional, Old Town Tokyo feel.

Locator Map
For more detail see p112 and p88

0 meters   400
0 yards   400   N↑

*In the spring, cherry blossom (sakura) trees flower along the banks of the **Kanda River**.*

*Finish in the famous **Jimbocho Booksellers' District** (p99).*

*Look out for **Casals Hall**, an auditorium designed by architect Arata Isozaki.*

One of many bookshops in the Jimbocho Bookseller's District

*Start at **Yushima Tenjin Shrine**, dedicated to a 9th-century scholar deified as Tenjin, the patron of learning.*

Kyu Iwasaki-tei Mansion

Yushima S

KASUGA-DORI

Uenohirokoji S

Yushima Tenjin Shrine
START

SHOHEIBASHI-DORI

UENO

CHUO-DORI

YUSHIMA

3331 Arts Chiyoda

KARAMAEBASHI-DORI

Suehirocho S

Kanda Myojin Shrine

YUSHIMA-ZAKA

SOTOKANDA

Yushima Seido Temple

Ochanomizu

AIOI-ZAKA

Nikolai Cathedral

KANDA AWAJICHO

Kanda Yabu Soba

S Shin-ochanomizu

S Awajicho

S Ogawamachi

DORI

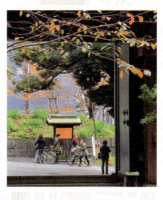

↑ Entrance of Yushima Seido Temple, dedicated to Confucius

Kanda Myojin Shrine (p108), *dates back over 1,250 years. Its bi-annual festival is one of Tokyo's most important Shinto events.*

*Across the road is **Yushima Seido Temple**, dedicated to the spirit of the Chinese sage Confucius. Shady temple gardens are situated at the base of a bluff above the banks of the Kanda River.*

*Stop for lunch at **Kanda Yabu Soba**, a legendary buckwheat noodle restaurant that has been running here since 1880.*

*The deep green domes of the Russian Orthodox **Nikolai Cathedral** are an interesting contrast to the rest of the Tokyo cityscape.*

→ Nikolai Cathedral, also known as the Holy Resurrection Cathedral

A LONG WALK
YANAKA

Distance 2 miles (3.5 km) **Walking time** 50 minutes
Terrain An easy route through city streets **Nearest station** Nishi-Nippori Metro Station

This walk takes in the neighborhoods of Yanaka (*p126*) and Nezu. Along with Sendagi to the west, this area is known as Yanesen (a portmanteau of the three names). Having survived both the Great Kanto Earthquake of 1923 and the fire bombings of World War II relatively unscathed, Yanesen is one of the best-preserved old quarters of Tokyo, and a walk here offers a chance to see a rare enclave of the old city. Highlights of Yanaka include the cemetery, a tranquil space full of mossy tombs, stone Buddha statues, and cherry trees where a number of famous literati, actors, and former Shoguns have been laid to rest. Nezu is another one of Tokyo's Shitamachi (Low City) old town districts, whose narrow streets do not allow for heavy traffic and are ideal for walking. The most famous sight here is the Nezu Shrine, which has a long tunnel of *torii* gates that feels like the pathway to the spirit world.

Locator Map
For more detail see p112

Take a detour here for a tea break in the narrow shopping street known as the **Yanaka Ginza**.

At **Daien-ji Temple**, two adjoining halls – one Shinto, one Buddhist – have fine wooden carvings of dragons, nymphs, and phoenixes.

Across the road from Daien-ji is one of Tokyo's oldest and most exquisite paper arts shops, **Isetatsu**, where you can view fans, combs and dolls.

Sendagi [S] Daien-ji Temple

Isetatsu

0 meters 400
0 yards 400
N ↑

SENDAGI

SHINOBAZU - DORI

NICHI-IDAI-TSUTSUJI-DORI

FINISH
Nezu Shrine

NEZU

SHINOBAZU - DORI

Todaimae [S]

YAYOI

Nezu [S]

KOTOTOI-DORI

Enter **Nezu Shrine** through the impressive romon gate, then to a second portal, Karamon gate, with some fine lacquered partitions.

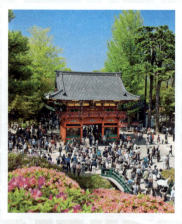

↑ Visitors around the Nezu Shrine's two-storied *romon* (tower agte)

Tenno-ji temple's
17th-century bronze
Buddha statue

START
Nishi-Nippori
Station

Suwa Shrine

Joko-ji Temple

NISHI-
NIPPORI

Yofukuji-ji Temple

Kyoo-ji
Temple

Nippori

SUWADAI STREET

YANAKA GINZA

Asakura
Museum
of Sculpture

Zensho-an
Temple

Tenno-ji Temple

Yanaka
Cemetery

YANAKA

SCAI –
The Bathhouse

Ueno Sakuragi
Atari

Daimyo
Clock Museum

KOTOTOI-DORI

Hantei

Tenno-ji Temple adjoins the
cemetery grounds. Its focal
point is a statue of the Great
Buddha of Yanaka, a bronze
figure cast in 1691.

With its shaded paths, wrought-
iron gates, and worn stone
lanterns, **Yanaka Cemetery**
has a Gothic character.

Turn right down Sansakizaka to find
Zenshoan Temple. Meditation
sessions are held here on Sunday
mornings, but the main point of
interest is a tall, gold-leaf-covered
statue in the main hall; this is known
as the Yanaka Kannon, after
the goddess of mercy.

The **Daimyo Clock Museum**
displays a fascinating collection
of timepieces made exclusively
for Japan's feudal lords.

Cross Kototoi-dori
until you see a unique
three-story wooden
Meiji-era building
that houses **Hantei**,
an atmospheric
kushiage (deep-fried
food) restaurant.

A dusting of cherry
blossom petals in
Yanaka Cemetery

Must See

❶ Toyosu Fish Market

Experience More

❷ Gotoh Museum
❸ Japan Folk Crafts Museum
❹ Ikebukuro
❺ Toden-Arakawa Tram Line
❻ Ebisu
❼ Sengaku-ji
❽ Ghibli Museum
❾ Shimokitazawa
❿ Daikanyama
⓫ Gokoku-ji Temple
⓬ Fukagawa
⓭ Kyu Furukawa Garden
⓮ Zoshigaya Cemetery
⓯ Rikugi-en Garden
⓰ Ryogoku
⓱ Odaiba

BEYOND THE CENTER

Tokyo is by far the biggest urban area in the world, but don't feel daunted by the city's size – exploring beyond the center poses few problems thanks to Tokyo's superb transportation system, and it's well worth heading off the beaten path to visit the outer-districts. Not only do they offer a breath of fresh air from the frenetic inner city, but each area is full of personality – whether it's the pop culture hot spot of Ikebukuro, the sumo center of Ryogoku, or the hip and musical Shimokitazawa. Here, too, you'll find some of the city's most exciting modern developments, such as the vast fish market at Toyosu, and the futuristic, man-made island of Odaiba.

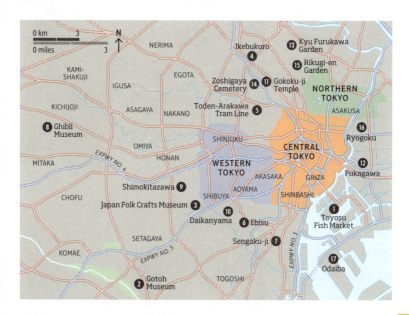

❶

TOYOSU FISH MARKET

豊洲市場

🏠 6-6-2 Toyosu, Koto-ku 🚇 Shijo-mae

The largest market of its kind in the world and the beating heart of Japan's gastronomic culture, the Toyosu fish market turns over some 1,200 tons of seafood every single day. Most visitors come here not to buy fish, but to soak up vibrant market life and to eat the freshest sushi.

After years of delays, this state-of-the-art fish market opened in 2018 in Toyosu, just 1 mile (2 km) away from the previous site at Tsukiji. Sleeker and less chaotic than its predecessor, Toyosu's purpose-designed layout eliminates previous tensions between tourists and market traders. Head to the observation deck to watch the daily tuna auction below (book in advance).

This takes place from 4:30am, and lasts up to an hour, with huge fish laid out in long rows for buyers. While visitors are not able to purchase directly from the market, many sushi vendors that plied their trade in the shadow of the old Tsukiji market have also made the move over to Toyosu, providing hungry visitors with some of the freshest sushi imaginable.

TUNA FISH SUPPLIES

Toyosu specializes in *maguro* (tuna) from as far away as New Zealand and the North Atlantic. The Japanese consume about 30 per cent of the annual global 1.7 million-ton tuna catch, and eat 80 per cent of tuna raw, as sashimi, which requires the best cuts of fish. The Pacific Ocean's South Blue Fin tuna, a favorite for sashimi, is declining steadily in spite of efforts to manage numbers. The Japanese fishing industry has come under a great deal of scrutiny, with other governments exerting pressure on Japan to keep an eye on its activities.

→

Bustling stalls laden with fresh fish in the Toyosu Fish Market

1 Market traders can be seen slicing fish using a huge knife requiring two people. Cutting the fish in this way serves to demonstrate its freshness to potential buyers.

2 Buyers browse tuna fish before bidding on them.

3 As well as fish, Toyosu's traders sell fruit and vegetables, such as wasabi, in a designated area.

Did You Know?

The tuna auction area is cooled down to almost 32° F (0° C) – bring a sweater!

↑ A skilled chef preparing different kinds of sushi at a restaurant in Tokyo

SUSHI AND SASHIMI

Newcomers to Japan are often both fascinated and intimidated by these ubiquitous dishes. While sashimi denotes sliced fillets of raw fish served without rice, there are several different types of sushi (usually written with the suffix "-zushi") in which cold, lightly sweetened, and vinegared rice is topped or wrapped up with raw fish or other items, such as pickles or cooked meat.

NIGIRI-ZUSHI

Thin slices of raw fish are laid over molded fingers of rice with a thin layer of wasabi in between. Dip it in soy sauce, and consume in one mouthful.

CHIRASHI-ZUSHI

The "scattered" style involves a colorful combination of toppings, including fish, chunks of omelet, and vegetables, artfully arranged on a deep bed of cold rice.

MAKI-ZUSHI

"Rolled" sushi is very familiar outside Japan. Rice is combined with slivers of fish and other morsels, and rolled up in a sheet of toasted seaweed (nori).

SASHIMI

Sliced fillets of the freshest uncooked fish may be served alone. Sashimi is delicate and creamy, and the only accompaniments should be soy sauce, wasabi, daikon, and maybe a shiso leaf.

POPULAR FISH IN JAPAN

Of the 3,000 or so varieties of seafood eaten in Japan, the most common are maguro (tuna), tai (sea bream), buri (yellowtail), saba (mackerel), sake (salmon), tara (cod), and crustaceans such as ebi (shrimp) and kani (crab). You'll find these fish on menus and in market stalls all year round, but some fish are seasonal treats. In spring, there's ayu (sweet-fish), a river fish traditionally caught by trained cormorants. Katsuo (skipjack tuna) is best in spring and summer, unagi (eel) in mid-summer, and sanma (saury) in the fall. Winter is the time for dojo (loach), anko (angler fish), and fugu (blowfish), prized for its delicate flavor but also feared for deadly toxins in its liver and ovaries.

EXPERIENCE MORE

2

Gotoh Museum
五島美術館

 3-9-25 Kaminoge, Setagaya ☎(03) 5777-8600 🚃 Kaminoge ⏰10am–5pm Tue–Sun

Set in a pleasant hillside garden, this museum showcases the private collection of the late chairman of the Tokyu Corporation, Keita Gotoh. He was originally attracted to Buddhist calligraphy (*bokuseki*), and his collection contains many examples of this work. Also included are ceramics, paintings, and metalwork mirrors.

The museum's most famous works, however, are a set of 12th-century scrolls featuring scenes from the *Tale of Genji*, painted by Fujiwara Takayoshi, which have been designated

Did You Know?

The *Tale of Genji*, by Lady Murasaki, is thought to be the world's first novel.

National Treasures. They are shown once a year, usually during Golden Week (April 29–early May). The museum is closed during summer maintenance, when exhibitions change over.

3

Japan Folk Crafts Museum
日本民芸館

🏠 4-3-33 Komaba, Meguro 🚃 Komaba-Todaimae ⏰10am–4:30pm Tue–Sun 🌐 mingeikan.or.jp

Known to the Japanese as Mingeikan (*mingei* meaning "folk crafts"), this small but excellent museum was set up by art historian Soetsu Yanagi. Yanagi valued the simple and utilitarian nature of hand-made, everyday objects, and started the *mingei* movement to preserve such designs in the era of mass-production. The criteria for inclusion in the museum's collection are that the object should be the work of an anonymous maker, produced for daily use, and representative of the region from which it comes. On display are a huge variety of items,

including woven baskets to axe sheaths, iron kettles, pottery, and kimonos. There are also themed exhibits, such as 20th-century ceramics, tie-dye techniques or Japanese textiles, and a room dedicated to Korean Yi-dynasty work. A small gift shop sells fine crafts.

DRINK

Belg Aube Toyosu
A café with a good range of Belgian beers and European dishes.

🏠 LaLaport Toyosu 1F, 2-4-9 Toyosu, Koto ☎(03) 6910-1275

Hops125
One of Tokyo's most exciting craft beer venues, Hops125 features a diverse array of local and international beers, with more than 10 on tap at any time.

🏠 1 Chome-21-18 Ebisu, Shibuya ☎(03) 3447-1496

Spring Balley Brewing
The beers on tap at this cool brewpub include everything from crisp pils and IPAs to experimental fruit beers.

🏠 Log Road Daikanyama, Daikanyamacho, Shibuya ☎(03) 6416-4960

 ←

Exterior of the Japan Folk Crafts Museum, designed by its art-historian founder

❹

Ikebukuro
池袋

🚌 & Ⓢ **Ikebukuro**

Ikebukuro has become one of Japan's most popular *otaku* (geek) districts. Here you'll find the flagship store for the country's biggest anime goods retailer – Animate – as well as several locations of their Animate Cafe, where the anime-themed decor, menu, and exclusive merchandise change every few months.

While Tokyo's most famous geek district, Akihabara *(p96)*, is more popular with men, Ikebukuro is frequented mostly by women, as many of the stores in the area focus on media with a large female fanbase. The district even has a butler café *(www.butlers-cafe.jp)* in place of Akihabara's typical maid versions.

But even non-*otaku* will enjoy exploring this lively leisure district, which is full of shops, arcades, bars, and restaurants. Thre's also the incredible **Sunshine City** mall, which has an aquarium, observation deck, and amusement park, plus a long list of stores and restaurants. With all of this activity, the Ikebukuro district has firmly earned a spot on the map of cool Tokyo highlights.

Sunshine City
🏠 3-Chome-1 Higashi-ikebukuro ⏰ Times vary, see website 🌐 sunshinecity.jp

---

❺

Toden-Arakawa Tram Line
荒川都電

🚉 **Many stations**

In 1955, 600,000 people a day were riding the dozens of tram lines that crisscrossed the city. Now the 8-mile-(13-km-) Toden-Arakawa line is one of only two that remain, along with the privately-owned Tokyu Setagaya line. The others were eliminated as old-fashioned in the modern-ization for the 1964 Olympics.

The Toden-Arakawa line runs from Waseda in the west to Minowabashi in the east and costs ¥170 for each trip. The tram itself is a Tokyo highlight, and there are also lots of interesting places to explore along the route. Near the Waseda end of the line is the Higo-Hosokawa Teien stroll garden. A short walk from Arakawayuenchi-Mae stop is the Arakawa Yuen Amusement Park (closed for renovations until 2021). Opposite the Arakawa-Nanachome stop is the tranquil Arakawa Nature Park.

A tram trundling along the Arakawa Tram Line at night ↑

❻

Ebisu
恵比寿

🚌 & Ⓢ **Ebisu**

In 1994 the completion of Yebisu Garden Place – a commercial and residential center – brought this area to life. The **Tokyo Photographic Art Museum** has a permanent collection of work by Japanese and foreign photographers. In the center are a Mitsukoshi store, numerous boutiques, two cinemas, a theater, and restaurants. To the left of Mitsukoshi is the small **Yebisu Beer Museum** containing exhibits and videos about beer worldwide and in Japan, plus free samples.

Tokyo Photographic Art Museum
♿ 🏠 1-13-3 Mita, Meguro ⏰ 10am–6pm Tue–Sun (to 8pm) 🌐 topmuseum.jp

↑ The illuminated entrance gate to the Sunshine City mall, with its numerous restaurants and shops

Did You Know?

The Ebisu district was named after the Yebisu Beer brand.

SHOP

Yebisu Beer Museum

Ⓢ 📍 4-20-1 Ebisu, Shibuya 📞 (03) 5423-7255 🕙 11am–7pm Tue–Sun

---

⑦ Sengaku-ji
泉岳寺

📍 2-11-1 Takanawa, Minato Ⓢ Sengaku-ji 🕙 Museum: 9am–4:30pm daily (Oct–Mar: to 4pm) 🌐 sengakuji.or.jp

This is the site of the climax of Japan's favorite tale of loyalty and revenge, retold in the play *Chushingura* and many movies. Lord Asano was sentenced to death by seppuku (ritual disembowelment) for drawing his sword when goaded by Lord Kira. Denied the right to seek revenge, 47 of Asano's retainers (or *ronin*), led by Oishi Kuranosuke, plotted in secret. In 1702, they attacked and beheaded Kira, presenting the head to Asano's grave at Sengaku-ji. They in turn were sentenced to seppuku and are buried here. Inside the temple gate is the well where the *ronin* washed Kira's head. Farther ahead on the right are the retainers' graves. Back at the base of the steps is an interesting museum with artifacts from the incident, which you can visit for a fee.

Statue of *ronin* leader Oishi Kuranosuke at Sengaku-ji

⑧ Ghibli Museum
三鷹の森
ジブリ美術館

📍 1-Chome-1-83 Shimorenjaku, Mitaka 🚉 Mitaka 🕙 10am–6pm Wed–Mon 🌐 ghibli-museum.jp

Studio Ghibli is known throughout the world for its wonderful animated films – some of them charming coming-of-age tales, and others high fantasy epics. The museum makes fans feel as if they have stepped straight into a Ghibli setting, with the studio's trademark style and attention to detail evident throughout thr grounds. Among the many nooks and crannies to explore are the cinema showing short animated films exclusive to the museum, a fascinating replica of an animation studio, and a café with themed treats. Children will also enjoy letting off steam in the play area inspired by *My Neighbor Totoro*. Make sure to book your tickets well in advance.

Yebisu Garden Place, a chic commercial center in Ebisu

People enjoying the cool, alternative vibe of the Shimokitazawa district

9

Shimokitazawa
下北沢

 Shimokitazawa

More popularly known as Shimokita, one of the most distinguishing characteristics of this area is its cool, alternative atmosphere, giving Shimokita a reputation as a real hispter haven.

The seeds of the this relaxed image were sown in the 1960s when a number of small fringe theaters opened here. Some of these still operate today, and more have been added over the years to create a thriving drama scene. The best and most famous

---

> 💬 **INSIDER TIP**
> ### Shimokita's Coffee Shops
>
> Some coffee shops in Shimokitazawa celebrate the relaxed, social aspect of coffee breaks, and are great places to sit and people watch. Others take coffee so seriously that customers are forbidden from taking photos of their drinks.

---

venue is the **Honda Theater**, which provides small but convivial spaces for modern, experimental productions.

Shimokitazawa's north side is full of record stores, vintage clothing boutiques, and international restaurants. Its independent cafés are especially famous, earning fans from far and wide. The south side, meanwhile, is renowned as the trend-setting center of Tokyo's music scene. Home to an incredible number of music venues, this is the place to enjoy a Japanese institution known as the "live house". These intimate live music venues are where patrons come to enjoy music in peace, rather than to drink and socialise as at many other bars.

Honda Theater
🏠 2-10-15 Kitazawa
🌐 honda-geki.com

10

Daikanyama
代官山

 Daikanyama

An important archaeological site, where well-preserved burial mounds and ancient pit

dwellings have been discovered, Daikanyama is better known these days as a classy, low-rise neighborhood. It is more popular with the smart set, who come here to explore its trendy boutiques, restaurants, patisseries, and alfresco pavement cafés.

Some big name international fashion brands, such as Jean Paul Gaultier, have outposts here, adding more class and distinction to an already chic district. The area, with its back lanes, shops, and home courtyards full of greenery, makes for a pleasant stroll. Interest in the area first grew when Japanese architect Fumihiko Maki began his ongoing Hillside Terrrace, an apartment, gallery, and shopping project along leafy Kyu Yamate-dori, in 1969. Buildings have been added over the decades. The **Art Front Gallery** hosts interesting art exhibitions, while closer to the station Daikanyama Address Dixsept complex houses boutiques and trendy cafés. Another

→

Surprisingly little-visted Gokoku-ji, one of Edo's most important temples major addition came in 2011 with the multiple-design-award-winning **Daikanyama T-Site** complex, a sleek combination of book store, café and even dog salon, among other things.

Art Front Gallery
 (03) 3476-4868
🕐 11am-7pm Wed-Sun

Daikanyama T-Site
📞 (03) 3770-2525
🕐 7am-2am daily

11

Gokoku-ji Temple
護国寺

🚇 Gokoku-ji 📞 (03) 3941-0764

Little-visited Gokoku-ji is one of Edo's most important temples. Before entering the spacious grounds of the temple, visitors pass through the arresting Niomon gate. The gate takes its name from the statues of two fierce-looking, red-faced Deva kings positioned at either side of the entrance. The statues are meant to ward off malevolent spirits. The right-hand figure's mouth is open, while his companion's is closed. This symbolizes exhalation and inhalation, creation and dissolution; the harmony of opposites encountered in many of Japan's arts.

Stunningly well preserved, the complex's main hall, dating from 1681, with its sweeping copper roof and massive pillars, is a treasure house of Buddhist statuary. Foremost among the deities here are Kannon, the goddess of mercy. Eight celestial maidens dance across the ceiling in paintings that float over transoms covered with colorful carvings of peonies. Completing the ensemble of buildings that have been designated Important Cultural Properties are an imposing bell tower and a rare two-tiered pagoda, a popular subject for painters.

EAT

Tokyo Ramen Kokugi-kan
Six ramen shops offering Sapporo-style miso ramen, Hakata-style *tonkotsu* (pork bone) ramen, and more.

🏠 Aqua City Odaiba 5F, 1-7-1 Daiba, Minato
📞 (03) 3599-4700

Odaiba Takoyaki Museum
Stalls dish up variations on the classic fried batter and octopus balls, a regional dish from the southern city of Osaka.

🏠 Decks Tokyo Beach, 1-6-1 Daiba, Minato
🌐 odaiba-decks.com/en/takoyaki

¥¥¥

12

Fukagawa
深川

🚇 Monzen-Nakacho,
Kiyosumi-Shirakawa

This area is situated east of the Sumida River and squarely within what was known as Shitamachi. It took centuries to reclaim the land from Tokyo Bay and the estuary. To get a good historical grip on the neighborhood, visit the **Fukagawa Edo Museum**. It recreates an old area of Fukagawa circa 1840, with 11 original buildings, homes, shops, a theater, boathouse, tavern, and a 33-ft- (10-m-) high fire tower. The interiors of the houses have an authentic atmosphere with fishing nets and workmen's clothing casually hung on the walls, and empty shells strewn on the floor of a reproduced clam peddler's home.

Fukagawa has several lovely outdoor spaces to enjoy when you need a break from exploring the city streets.

First, spanning a vast space either side of the small Sendaibori River, Kiba Park is home to the **Museum of Contemporary Art**, which reopened in 2019 after undergoing major improvements. The rest of the park – with its botanic gardens, tennis courts, barbecue area, and lawns for strolling – is the ideal place to relax with the family. Only 15 minutes away, built within the

MATSUO BASHO

In 1680, Japan's most famous poet, Matsuo Basho (1644–94), moved to the then inaccessible backwater of Fukagawa. At that time, there were no bridges crossing the Sumida River, and Basho could finally escape his admiring public and achieve the isolation he needed to focus on his writing. It was Fukagawa that served as a base for some of his most famous journeys, and where he wrote his famous frog haiku.

grounds of a large estate in the area of present-day Kiyosumi Shirakawa, the **Kiyosumi Teien** is a beautifully landscaped garden. The grounds are a classic Edo-era *kaiyushiki teien*, or "pond walk around garden," with plants that bloom at different times of the year. A teahouse, which floats above the water, and 55 rare stones, brought from all over Japan by Mitsubishi steamships, are the highlights of this garden.

North of Kiyosumi Teien, the small nieghborhood of Kiyosumi has won fame for its many high-quality independent coffee shops. If you can't live without flat whites or pour over coffees, make sure to pay a visit to one of the many cafés here.

In nearby Monzen Nakacho, the Tomioka Hachiman-gu shrine dates from the 17th century. The current building is a 1968 reconstruction, but its prayer and spirit halls and the copper-tiled roof are very impressive. The famed Flea Market, the Fukagawa *ennichi*, is another attraction. This lively event is held in the shrine grounds on the first, second, and fourth Sundays of the month, from around 6am to sunset.

Fukagawa Edo Museum
🏠 1 Chome-3-28 Shirakawa, Koto 📞 (03) 3630-8625
🕐 9:30am–5pm daily 🚫 2nd & 4th Mon

Museum of Contemporary Art
♿ 🚻 🛍 🏠 4 Chome-1-1 Miyoshi, Koto 🕐 10am–6pm Tue–Sun 🌐 mot-art-museum.jp

Kiyosumi Teien
🏠 1 Chome-3-16 Kiyosumi, Koto 📞 (03) 3641-5892
🕐 9am–5pm daily

←
The charming Kyu Furukawa Teien house with its English-style rose garden

← The Fukagawa Edo Museum, which recreates an area of 19th-century Fukagawa

The small neighborhood of Kiyosumi in Downtown Fukagawa has gained a reputation as a haven for coffee lovers.

 13

Kyu Furukawa Garden
旧古河庭園

🏠 1 Chome-27-39 Nishigahara, Kita 🚇 & Ⓢ Komagome 🕐 9am–5pm daily 🌐 tokyo-park.or.jp/teien

In addition to Rikugi-en Garden (p148), the district of Komagome has another garden of note: Kyu Furukawa. Its main building, a charcoal-grey stone residence designed by British architect Josiah Conder in 1917, resembles a small Scottish manor house. To see the interior, you need to book in advance (www.otanimuseum.or.jp/kyufurukawatei).

The mansion and its English-style rose garden sit on a ridge above steps leading down to a landscaped area, replete with a tea-ceremony pavilion and a small waterfall that feeds into a heart-shaped pond.

 14

Zoshigaya Cemetery
雑司ヶ谷霊園

🏠 4 Chome-25-1 Minami-ikebukuro, Toshima 🚇 Ikebukuro Ⓢ Higashi-Ikebukuro 📞 (03) 3971-6868

Zoshigaya Cemetery is the resting place of several important literary figures, including Japanese novelists such as Soseki Natsume and Kafu Nagai. The Greek-Irish writer Lafcadio Hearn, whose books helped to introduce Japan to the West in the Meiji era, is also buried here. Scenic tree-endowed graveyards such as Zoshigaya can get crowded during the spring cherry-blossom-viewing season. Another little-visited spot, the **Zoshigaya Missionary Museum** built in 1907 by an American missionary John Moody McCaleb, is a very well-preserved colonial house, which is open to visitors.

Zoshigaya Missionary Museum

🏠 Zoshigaya 1-25-5 🕐 9am–4:30pm Tue-Sun

→ The grave of writer Natsume Souseki in Zoshigaya Cemetery

15 Rikugi-en Garden
六義園

& **S** Komagome **C** (03) 3941-2222 **O** 9am–5pm daily

Yanagisawa Yoshiyasu, grand chamberlain of the fifth shogun, built this garden, one of the finest Edo-era stroll gardens, in seven years, from 1695. The fine design recreates 88 landscapes in miniature from famous *waka* (31-syllable poems), so the view changes every few steps. Sit on one of the many seats and enjoy the views.

16 Ryogoku
両国

& **S** Ryogoku

A great entertainment and commerce center during the Edo era, Ryogoku is now a quiet place. However, it is still the best place to find the residents who have long made this district famous: sumo wrestlers. Many *beya* (sumo stables) are here, and it is not unusual to see the

athletes walking the streets in *yukata* (light cotton kimonos) and *geta* (wooden sandals).

The Kokugikan sumo arena also houses the **Sumo Museum**, which is lined with portraits of all the *yokozuna* (grand champions). Beside the stadium is the **Edo-Tokyo Museum**, one of Tokyo's most imaginative museums. Two zones trace life in Edo and then Tokyo, as Edo was renamed in 1868. The exhibits have explanations in Japanese and English. The route around the museum starts by crossing a traditional arched wooden bridge, a replica of Nihonbashi. There are life-sized reconstructed buildings, plus scale-model dioramas showing everything from the house of a daimyo (feudal lord) to a section of Shitamachi. Beside a scale model of Tokyo's first skyscraper is rubble from the 1923 earthquake. Models of the boats that once plied the Sumida River give an

↑ A bridge crossing a pond in the verdant Rikugi-en Garden

idea of just how important the river was to Edo life. In the media section is a step-by-step example of how ukiyo-e woodblock prints (*p150*) were produced.

The **Sword Museum** is full of fine Japanese swords, some dating back to the 12th century. There is also a display of decorated hilts and old Japanese texts, illustrated with beautiful drawings, explaining the finer points of sword-making.

Opened in 2016, **The Sumida Hokusai Museum** is devoted to the famous ukiyo-e artist Katsushika Hokusai – perhaps most famous for his print *The Great Wave off Kanagawa*. The museum has an amazing array of Hokusai's art as well as videos and multilingual information about the artist and his life.

Sumo Museum
1-3-28 Yokoami, Sumida
O 10am–4:30pm Mon–Fri
W sumo.or.jp

Edo-Tokyo Museum
1-4-1 Yokoami, Sumida
O 9:30am–5:30pm Tue–Sun (to 7:30pm Sat) **W** edo-tokyo-museum.or.jp

---

LIFE IN A SUMO STABLE

At the age of about 15, boys are accepted into a *beya*. Sumo society is supremely hierarchical, with newcomers serving senior wrestlers as well as cleaning and cooking for the entire *beya*. Junior practices may start at 4am. The day's single meal of *chanko-nabe*, a large stew, comes about noon, with juniors getting what the seniors leave. After, more work follows.

Sword Museum

 🏠1-12-9 Yokoami, Sumida
🕐9:30am–5pm Tue–Sun
🌐touken.or.jp

The Sumida
Hokusai Museum

🏠2 Chome 7-2
Kamezawa, Sumida
🕐9:30am–5:30pm Tue–Sun
🌐hokusai-museum.jp

17

Odaiba
お台場

🚉Odaiba-kaihinkoen
🚢From Hinode Pier
11:25am–6pm, every
40–50 mins

When the West began to force Japan to open up in the 1850s, the shogunate constructed a series of *daiba* (obstructions) across Tokyo harbor to keep the foreign ships out. Odaiba (sometimes known as Daiba), an island almost blocking the mouth of Tokyo Bay, takes its name from these. The spectacular route to Odaiba is via the Yurikamome monorail, which climbs a loop before joining Rainbow Bridge high over Tokyo Harbor.

The first station, Odaiba-Kaihin-Koen, leads to Tokyo's only beach. Nearby is the Daisan Daiba Historic Park, with the remains of the original obstructions. A short walk west is Decks Tokyo Beach, which has six floors of restaurants and shops plus Joypolis, a huge Sega center full of the latest electronic games. In front of Decks is the station for water buses from Hinode Pier. Located in Aomi, the **National Museum of Emerging Science and Innovation**, better known as Miraikan, has interactive robots, biotechnology, and ecological exhibits. The Fuji TV building dominates the area.

At Aomi station is the Palette Town development, including Venus Fort, a shopping mall whose interior recreates an 18th-century Italian town at twilight. Palette Town also includes Mega Web's Toyota City Showcase, with a massive display area, and state-of-the-art driving simulators. The Wanza Ariake building has shops and restaurants and is connected to Kokusai-Tenjijo Seimon station, as is Tokyo Big Sight (or Tokyo International Exhibition Hall).

National Museum
of Emerging Science
and Innovation (Miraikan)

🏠2-3-6 Aomi, Koto 🕐10am–5pm Wed–Mon 🔒Dec 28–Jan 1 🌐miraikan.jst.go.jp

STAY

Hotel Metropolitan
Tokyo Ikebukuro

Located at the center of the bustling Ikebukuro neighborhood, this is a relaxed and welcoming luxury hotel at an affordable price. Some rooms boast views of Mount Fuji.

🏠1-6-1 Nishiikebukuro, Toshima 🌐metropolitan.jp

Samurais Hostel
Ikebukuro

At this kitsch hostel, guests can enjoy classical Japanese art on the walls, as well as glow-in-the-dark samurai murals. Private rooms are also available if you don't want to share a dorm.

🏠3-52-12 Ikebukuro, Toshima 🌐hiromas.net

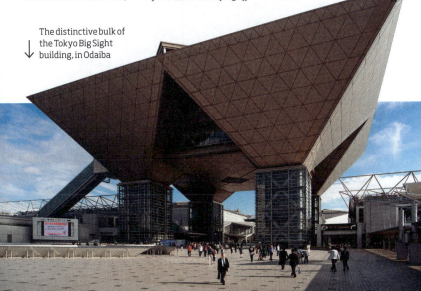

↓ The distinctive bulk of the Tokyo Big Sight building, in Odaiba

THE FLOATING WORLD OF UKIYO-E

During the Edo period (1603–1868), wood-block prints known as ukiyo-e became the most popular pictorial art of Japan. The name (meaning "pictures of the floating world") comes from the colorful scenes of Edo-Tokyo's pleasure districts often depicted in ukiyo-e.

THE RISE OF UKIYO-E

The first artist known by name was Hishikawa Moronobu (1618–94), whose clean drawing style set the standard for artists to follow. The transition from black-and-white techniques to color came with Suzuki Harunobu's full-color calendar of beautiful women, published in 1765. The calendar was a great success and attracted both financiers and artists to the medium. Tokyo (then known as Edo) was the center of ukiyo-e production and subject matter, inspiring scenes of daily city life as well as prints of famous Kabuki actors and sumo wrestlers.

When Japan eventually opened up to international trade after its Edo-era isolationism, ukiyo-e were also a big hit abroad, influencing Western art movements such as Impressionism and Art Nouveau, and artists such as Matisse, Manet, and Van Gogh.

↑ Kyoto-based woodblock artist and printer Mamoru Ichimura

MAKING UKIYO-E

Although today they are credited to individual artists, ukiyo-e prints were originally a cooperative effort. The publisher was responsible for financing and distributing the work; the artist produced a fine line drawing; the carver made a wooden block for each color in the image; and the printer created the final product, inking the blocks and pressing them onto the paper – one for each color, starting with the lightest. In the 20th century, artists began to take control of every stage of the process, allowing *ukiyo-e* to become more personal and expressive than the original commercial prints.

Did You Know?

Ukiyo-e prints were usually limited to editions of 100–200 copies

A carving from artist Mamoru Ichimura's ↑ ukiyo-e studio

THEMES OF UKIYO-E

At the bottom of Edo-Tokyo's social hierarchy, the *chonin* (merchant) class developed their own distinct entertainment culture in pleasure quarters known as *ukiyo* (the "floating world"). Scenes from these vibrant and bawdy districts were the original subjects (and namesake) of ukiyo-e, but by the golden age of the medium (around 1790–1850), a number of other themes had become popular, common topics of ukiyo-e.

1. Women

Bijin-ga – images of Japanese beauties – were common throughout the development of ukiyo-e. Over-the-top, erotic images (*shun-ga*) were also popular, and some considered them to be good luck charms.

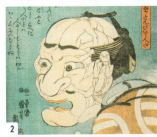

2. Humor

Toba-e were humorous caricatures. While these prints were not as prevalent at the time, their legacy is seen in the style, characters, and comedy of early manga.

3. Landscapes

Picturesque landscape views (*meisho-e*) allowed the public to see famous Japanese sights and scenery in an age when few could travel to see the country themselves.

4. History

Some of the most vibrantly-colored and detailed prints were those depicting famous samurai, historic battles, and scenes from traditional literature.

5. Celebrities

As stars of the pleasure districts where ukiyo-e was born, celebrities such as Kabuki actors and sumo wrestlers were often the subjects of commercial prints (*yakusha-e*).

1 *Three Beauties of the Present Day* (c 1792), a famous *bijin-ga* by artist Kitagawa Utamaro.

2 A *toba-e* by Utagawa Kuniyoshi (c 1850s), comically-titled *Looks fierce but he is a kind person*.

3 A print from Utagawa Hiroshige's landscape series *The Fifty-Three Stations of the Tokaido*, published between 1833–1834.

4 Yang Lin, a famous character from Chinese literature, as depicted by Utagawa Kuniyoshi (c 1822–35).

5 A 19th century print of a sumo match, by Kuniaki Hachisuka.

A LONG WALK
ODAIBA

Distance 4.5 miles (7 km) **Walking time** 90 minutes
Terrain An easy walk around a developed area
Nearest station Tokyo Big Sight

The post-modernist buildings, art installations, and fun attractions that constitute Odaiba (p149) make this man-made island feel like a quirky oasis plucked right out of wonderland. The flamboyant marriage of design, technology, commercialism, and leisure epitomizes Japan's fascination with blending high kitsch into a concoction that is both refined and brashly artificial. In this pleasure quarter for the city savvy, you'll find interesting museums, great leisure spots, and beautiful views of Toyo Bay all vying for your attention. You could easily spend the day here, but this walk will give you an introduction to the highlights.

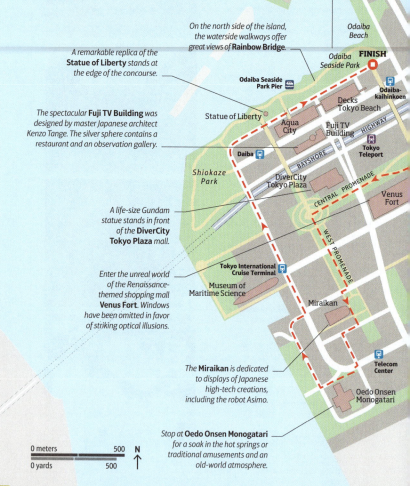

Odaiba Seaside Park is a pleasant sliver of green abutting a sandy, artificial beach.

On the north side of the island, the waterside walkways offer great views of Rainbow Bridge.

A remarkable replica of the Statue of Liberty stands at the edge of the concourse.

The spectacular Fuji TV Building was designed by master Japanese architect Kenzo Tange. The silver sphere contains a restaurant and an observation gallery.

A life-size Gundam statue stands in front of the DiverCity Tokyo Plaza mall.

Enter the unreal world of the Renaissance-themed shopping mall Venus Fort. Windows have been omitted in favor of striking optical illusions.

The Miraikan is dedicated to displays of Japanese high-tech creations, including the robot Asimo.

Stop at Oedo Onsen Monogatari for a soak in the hot springs or traditional amusements and an old-world atmosphere.

Odaiba Beach

FINISH

Odaiba Seaside Park

Odaiba-kaihinkoen

Odaiba Seaside Park Pier

Decks Tokyo Beach

Statue of Liberty

Aqua City

Fuji TV Building

Daiba

Tokyo Teleport

Shiokaze Park

DiverCity Tokyo Plaza

CENTRAL PROMENADE

Venus Fort

WEST PROMENADE

Tokyo International Cruise Terminal

Museum of Maritime Science

Miraikan

Telecom Center

Oedo Onsen Monogatari

DAIBA HIGHWAY

HIGHWAY

BAYSHORE

0 meters   500
0 yards   500

N

↑ Visitors admiring the view of the Statue of Liberty and Rainbow Bridge

Tokyo Water Science Museum

EAST PROMENADE

BAYSHORE

HIGHWAY

Kokusai-tenjijo

Ariake

Tokyo Big Sight

Tokyo Big Sight Pier

Tokyo Big Sight
START

One of Tokyo's prominent architectural marvels, **Tokyo Big Sight** *combines a convention center, cafés, and restaurants in a pyramidal structure that appears to be upside down.*

Giant Sky Wheel

Palette Town

Odaiba Pier

Aomi

Ride the **Giant Sky Wheel** *for great views of the picturesque Tokyo Bay.*

The **Palette Town** *complex is home to the teamLab Borderless, an innovative digital art gallery.*

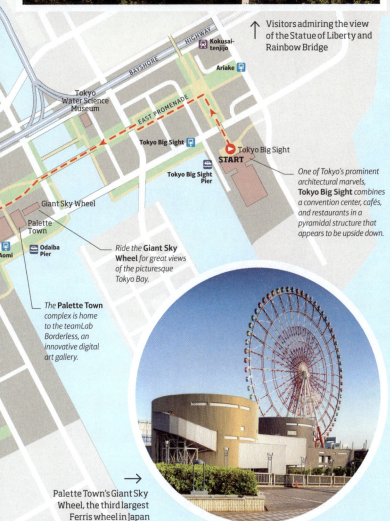

→ Palette Town's Giant Sky Wheel, the third largest Ferris wheel in Japan

BEYOND TOKYO

Some of Japan's most famous sights are just a short train or coach ride away from Tokyo, so don't hesitate to add a few day trips from the city to your itinerary. At the top of the list should be a visit to one of Japan's historic temple towns. Kamakura is a treasure-house of spectacular Zen temples, tranquil gardens, teahouses, and exquisite craft shops. And just a few hours north of Tokyo, the elaborate shrines, grand gates, and tombs of Nikko are overshadowed by towering forests of Japanese cedar, creating a mood of spiritual grandeur.

For a more cosmopolitan experience, the vibrant port city of Yokohama has a completely different feel to its neighbor Tokyo; the influence of its many foreign residents make it a real melting pot of a city. Nature lovers, meanwhile, will have plenty to enjoy in the regions around Tokyo. Hakone is the best place to go if you're eager for a traditional hot spring experience, while fine hiking trails, cycling routes, and wildlife are easily accessed at Chichibu-Tama-Kai National Park, the Izu Peninsula, and the Fuji Five Lakes. It's here that you'll find some of the best photo ops of Mount Fuji, one of the most iconic and breathtaking sights in all of Japan.

BEYOND TOKYO

Must Sees

1 Yokohama
2 Kamakura
3 Mount Fuji
4 Fuji Five Lakes
5 Nikko

Experience More

6 Narita
7 Kawagoe
8 Hakone
9 Izu Peninsula
10 Shizuoka
11 Katsunuma
12 Chichibu-Tama-Kai National Park
13 Suntory Hakushu Distillery

↑ The modern skyline of Yokohama's Minato Mirai 21 district

1

YOKOHAMA

横浜

 Kanagawa Prefecture **1-Chome-16-1, Takashima, Nishi; www.yokohamajapan.com**

Japan's second-largest city, Yokohama has been a center for shipping, trade, foreign contact, and modern ideas since the mid-19th century. Formerly a small fishing village on the Tokaido road, it was made a treaty port in 1859; there followed an influx of foreign traders, making it the biggest port in Asia by the early 1990s.

1

Landmark Tower

2-2-1 Minato Mirai
10am–9pm daily
yokohama-landmark.jp

Landmark Tower is the focal point of the futuristic Minato Mirai 21 district, an area of redeveloped docks that is particularly lively at the weekend. Built in 1993 under US architect Hugh Stubbins, the tower is Japan's fourth-tallest structure at 971 ft (296 m). Reached by the world's fastest elevator, traveling at 2,500 ft (750 m) per minute, the 69th-floor public lounge has a spectac-ular 360-degree view. Within the tower is the enormous Landmark Plaza shopping mall, which houses a numberof luxury brands, anime stores, and restaurants.

2

Yokohama Museum of Art

3-4-1 Minato Mirai
10am–6pm Fri–Wed
yokohama.art.museum

Yokohama's role as a meeting point between East and West means that it has long been a hub for the exchange of ideas. The Yokohama Museum of Art, designed by Kenzo Tange, celebrates this legacy with its impressive collection of modern art and photography. The museum is highly engaged with Yokohama itself, and focuses on Japanese artists with connections to the city, including Imamura Shiko, Kanzan Shimomura, and Chizuko Yoshida.

3

NYK Maritime Museum

3-9 Kaigandori **10am–5pm Tue–Sun** **nyk.com**

Founded in the 1880s, Nippon Yusen Kaisha (NYK) is one of the world's largest shipping companies. The quirky NYK Maritime Museum – with its exquisitely detailed model ships – celebrates the com-pany's history and Yokohama's connection to the sea, showing how maritime commerce has revolutionized marine technol-ogy, trade, and politics. Visitors are also provided with a free tea ceremony.

 HIDDEN GEM
Oodles of Noodles

True ramen obsessives should make a stop at Yokohama's Cup Noodles Museum (www.cup noodles-museum.jp), where visitors can fry their own ramen and design their own cup.

④
Hikawa Maru

🏠 Yamashita Park 🕐 10am-5pm Tue-Sun 🌐 nyk.com

Originally built in 1930 as a cruise liner and light cargo ship, the Hikawa Maru spent World War II operating as a floating hospital and in its 30 years of service crossed the Pacific 254 times, carrying some 25,000 passengers. The restored liner is now permanently docked in Yokohama, where visitors can stroll the decks, inspect the elegant wood-panelled cabins and soak up the Art Deco glamour of the lounge. Those who are technically minded will enjoy the opportunity to get close to the vessel's mighty engines.

Did You Know?

Japan's first railroad was constructed in 1872, connecting Yokohama to Tokyo.

⑤
Kantei-byo Temple

🏠 140 Yamashitacho 🕐 9am-7pm daily 🌐 yokohama-kanteibyo.com

Few sites better evoke Yokohama's cosmopolitan roots than Kantei-byo, the temple that has served as the heart of the city's Chinese community – the largest in Japan – for the past 150 years. The temple is dedicated to the ancient Chinese hero Emperor Guan, who is worshiped as a deity of business. This popular temple functions as a spiritual, cultural, and social hub, and is particularly atmospheric during Chinese New Year.

⑥
Yokohama Foreign General Cemetery

🏠 96 Yamatecho 🕐 10am-5pm Tue-Sun 🌐 yfgc-japan.com

Often called "Foreigners' Cemetery", this graveyard was founded in 1854 following the death of an American marine.

Among the 4,500 tombs is that of Edmund Morel, the English engineer who helped build Japan's first railroads.

⑦
Sankei-en Garden

🏠 58 Honmokusannotani 🕐 9am-5pm daily 🌐 sankeien.or.jp

With its ponds, bamboo groves, rivers, and meandering trails, this hideaway transports visitors back to ancient Japan. Among the garden's architectural treasures is a 15th-century pagoda, which was constructed in Kyoto and relocated to Sankei-en in 1914.

Opened to the public in 1906, the entire garden was once the private home of Tomitaro "Sankei" Hara (1868-1939), an extremely wealthy silk merchant. His personal lodgings – a sprawling complex featuring dozens of traditional tatami rooms, overlooking a private lawn – can be toured at the site.

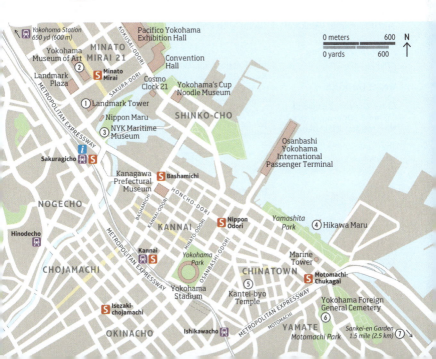

↑ Sagami Bay and rooftops of Kamakura houses from Hase-dera Temple

❷

KAMAKURA

鎌倉

🏠 Kanagawa Prefecture 🚉 🚌 ℹ️ At Kamakura Stn; www.city.kamakura.kanagawa.jp/kamakura-kankou

A seaside town of temples and wooded hills, Kamakura was Japan's administrative capital from 1192 until 1333. Favored by artists and writers, Kamakura has numerous antique and crafts shops, and in cherry-blossom season and on summer weekends, it teems with visitors.

①

Great Buddha

🏠 4-2-28 Hase 🚉 Hase 🚌 🕐 8am-5:30pm daily (Oct-Mar: to 5pm) 🌐 kotoku-in.jp

The Great Buddha (Daibutsu) is Kamakura's most famous sight. Cast in 1252, the bronze

---

Did You Know?

The Great Buddha has shock absorbers in its base to protect it from earthquakes.

---

statue of the Amida Buddha is 44 ft (13.5 m) tall. Its proportions are distorted so that it seems balanced to those in front of it – this use of perspective may show Greek influence (via the Silk Road).

②

Hase-dera Temple

🏠 3-11-2 Hase 🚉 Hase 🚌 🕐 8am-5:30pm daily (Oct-Feb: to 5pm) 🌐 hasedera.jp

Simple and elegant, Hase-dera is home to a superb 11-faced Kannon, bodhisattva of mercy. The Treasure House displays characterful Muromachi-era carvings of the 33 incarnations

---

💬 INSIDER TIP
Getting Around

Some parts of the town are best explored on foot but, with so many hills, it's worth buying a one-day bus pass from Kamakura station. The energetic can also rent a bicycle from here.

of Kannon. There is also a sutra repository; rotating the sutras is said to earn as much merit as reading them.

The 1264 bell is the town's oldest. Below it is a hall dedicated to Jizo, guardian of children, surrounded by countless statues to children who have died or been aborted.

---

③

Myohon-ji

🏠 1-15-1 Omachi 🚉 Kamakura 🕐 9am-5pm daily 🌐 myohonji.or.jp

On a hillside of soaring trees, this temple, with its unusually steep, extended roof, is the town's largest belonging to the Nichiren Buddhism sect. It was established in 1260, in memory of a 1203 massacre against the Hiki clan.

④ Tsurugaoka Hachiman-gu Shrine

📍 2-1-31 Yukinoshita
🚉 Kamakura ⏰ Shrine: 5am–9pm daily; Museum: 9am–4:30pm Tue–Sun (Oct–Mar: 6am–4:30pm)
🌐 tsurugaoka-hachiman gu.jp

Japan's Hachiman shrines are dedicated to the god of war; this one is also a guardian shrine of the Minamoto (or Genji) clan. Built in 1063 beside the sea, it was later moved here in 1191, and reconstructed in 1828. The approach runs between two lotus ponds: the Genji Pond has three islands (in Japanese *san* means both three and life) while the Heike Pond, named for a rival clan, has four (*shi* means both four and death). To the south, the Kamakura National Treasure House Museum contains a wealth of temple treasures.

---

⑤ Zuisen-ji

📍 710 Nikaido 🚌 ⏰ 9am–5pm daily 🌐 kamakura-zuisenji.or.jp

This secluded temple is known for its naturalistic garden. Created in 1327 by the monk Muso Soseki, it features a waterfall-fed lake, rocks, and sand; a Zen meditation cave is cut into the cliff. Decorative narcissi also bloom here in January, and Japanese plum trees blossom in February making it an idyllic natural oasis even before the cherry trees bloom.

→

The *hongu* (main hall) of the ornate Tsurugaoka Hachiman-gu Shrine

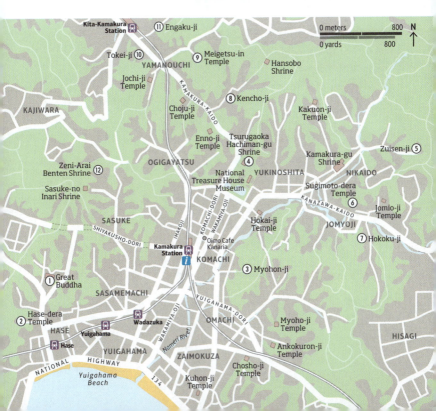

⑥
Sugimoto-dera Temple

⌂ 903 Nikaido ☎ (0467) 22-3463 🚌 ⏰ 8am-4:30pm daily

Founded in 734, this is the oldest temple in Kamakura, and pleasantly informal. The softly thatched hall contains three wooden statues of 11-faced Kannon, protected by ferocious guardian figures at the temple gateway.

---

⑦
Hokoku-ji

⌂ 2-7-4 Jomyoji ☎ (0467) 22-0762 🚌 ⏰ 9am-4pm daily

This Rinzai Zen temple was founded in 1334 and boasts a lovely bamboo grove, which you can visit for a fee, as well as a pleasant rock garden. The temple's Sunday-morning zazen (meditation) sessions are open to all.

> **Kencho-ji's beautiful rear garden is constructed around a pond supposedly in the shape of the kanji character for heart or mind.**

⑧
Kencho-ji

⌂ 8 Yamanouchi ☎ (0467) 22-0981 🚉 Kita-Kamakura ⏰ 8:30am-4:30pm daily

Kencho-ji is the foremost of Kamkura's "five great" Zen temples, and the oldest Zen training monastery in Japan. Founded in 1253, the temple originally had seven main buildings and 49 subtemples; many were destroyed in fires, but ten subtemples remain. Beside the impressive Sanmon Gate is the bell, cast in 1255, which has a Zen inscription by the temple's founder. The Buddha Hall contains a Jizo bodhisattva, savior of souls of the dead. Behind the hall is the Hatto, where public ceremonies are performed.

The Karamon (Chinese gate) leads to the Hojo, used for services. Kencho-ji's beautiful rear garden is constructed around a pond supposedly in the shape of the kanji character for heart or mind. To the side of the temple, a tree-lined lane leads to subtemples and up steps to Hanso-bo – the temple's shrine.

---

⑨
Meigetsu-in Temple

⌂ 1-8-9 Yamanouchi ☎ (0467) 24-3437 🚉 Kita-Kamakura ⏰ 9am-4pm daily (Jun: 8:30am-5pm)

Known as the "hydrangea temple," Meigetsu-in is a small Zen temple with

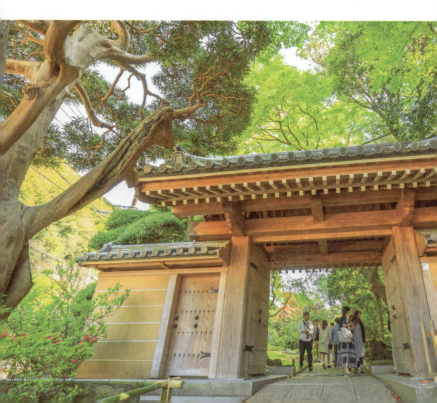

pretty gardens. As well as hydrangeas – which are at their peak in June – there are irises that bloom in late May, when the rear garden, usually only tantalizingly glimpsed through a round window, is opened to the public.

Inside the grand Butsunichian, the mausoleum of the founder of Engaku-ji

 ⑩

Tokei-ji

🏠 1367 Yamanouchi
📞 (0467) 22-1663
🚃 Kita-Kamakura
🕐 8:30am–4:30pm daily

This quiet little temple was set up as a convent in 1285, at a time when only men were allowed to petition for divorce. If a woman spent three years in a convent she could divorce her husband. Thus Tokei-ji was known as the "divorce temple." In 1873 the law was changed to allow women to initiate divorce, and in 1902 Tokei-ji became a monastery. It is still refuge-like, its gardens stretching back to wooded hillside.

⑪

Engaku-ji

🏠 409 Yamanouchi
📞 (0467) 22-0478
🚃 Kita-Kamakura
🕐 8am–4:30pm daily

The largest of Kamakura's "five great" Zen temples, and set deep in trees, Engaku-ji was founded by the Hojo regent Tokimune in 1282. An influential *zazen* (meditation) center since the Meiji era, it now runs public courses.

Although much of Engaku-ji was destroyed by the 1923 Kanto Earthquake, 17 of its more than 40 subtemples remain, and careful rebuilding has ensured that it retains its characteristic Zen layout (*p165*). One of its highlights, in the Shozoku-in subtemple, is the Shariden, which houses the relics of the Buddha. Japan's finest example of Chinese Sung-style Zen architecture, it is open only at New Year but can be seen through a gate at other times. Farther on, the Butsunichian – the mausoleum of Engaku-ji's founder – serves *matcha* tea to visitors. This was the setting for Kawabata Yasunari's 1949 novel *Senbazuru* (Thousand Cranes).

← The main gate to Hokoku-ji, surrounded by bamboo forest

⑫

Zeni-Arai Benten Shrine

🏠 2-25-16 Sasuke 📞 (0467) 25-1081 🚃 Kamakura
🕐 8:30am–4:30pm daily

This popular shrine is dedicated to Benten, goddess of the arts and eloquence, and one of the "seven lucky gods" of folk religion. Hidden in a niche in the cliffs, it is approached through a small tunnel and a row of torii gates. These lead to a cave spring where visitors wash coins in the hope of doubling their value.

EAT

Oimo Cafe Kanaria

This eatery near Kamakura station serves up parfaits and *kakigori* (shaved ice with syrup). Try one of the classic flavors, such as green tea or adzuki bean.

🏠 1F Enomoto Bldg, 2-10-10 Komachi, Kamakura-shi, Kanagawa 248-0006 🕐 Dinner, Wed 🌐 oimocafe.exblog.jp

¥ ¥ ¥

BUDDHISM IN JAPAN

Since the first priests from mainland Asia brought Buddhism to Japan in the 6th century, usurping the native Shinto, hundreds of separate Buddhist movements, sects, and subsects developed in the country. Contrasting beliefs appealed to different groups of nobility, samurai, and commoners, who each adapted practices to their own ends. In the eyes of many visitors today, Zen, one-time favorite of the samurai, is the quintessential religion of Japan, but it is just one of several major movements, and is itself subdivided into various sects. Of the other movements, the Tendai and Shingon sects of esoteric Buddhism still have millions of devotees.

ZEN BUDDHISM

This school developed during the Kamakura period (1185–1333). There are three main sects: Soto, Rinzai, and Obaku. All place emphasis on *zazen* (sitting meditation) and self-help.

TENDAI

Brought to Japan in the 9th century by the monk Saicho, Tendai places emphasis on selfless devotion. From its base at Mount Hiei, Tendai spawned the Jodo, Jodo Shin, and Nichiren sects.

SHINGON

Founded in Japan in the 9th century by the monk Kukai, this branch incorporates Hindu elements, such as hand gestures *(mudra)* and the chanting of mantras.

SHUGENDO

This offshoot of Shingon combines philosophies from Buddhism, Shinto, and Taosim, and promotes ascetic practices on mountain retreats.

The contemplative bronze figure of the Great Buddha in Kamakura ↑

↑ Senso-ji temple once belonged to the Tendai sect but is now a Sho-Kannon temple

THE LAYOUT OF A ZEN BUDDHIST TEMPLE

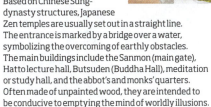

Designed to facilitate the path to englightenment, Zen Buddhist temples transport worshippers from the earthly world to that of the Buddha. Based on Chinese Sung-dynasty structures, Japanese Zen temples are usually set out in a straight line. The entrance is marked by a bridge over a water, symbolizing the overcoming of earthly obstacles. The main buildings include the Sanmon (main gate), Hatto lecture hall, Butsuden (Buddha Hall), meditation or study hall, and the abbot's and monks' quarters. Often made of unpainted wood, they are intended to be conducive to emptying the mind of worldly illusions.

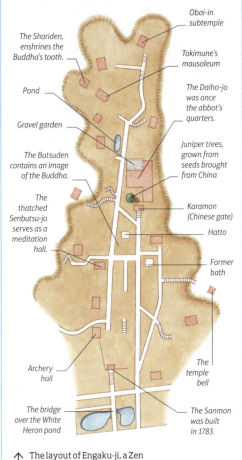

Obai-in subtemple

The Shariden, enshrines the Buddha's tooth.

Tokimune's mausoleum

Pond

The Daiho-jo was once the abbot's quarters.

Gravel garden

The Butsuden contains an image of the Buddha.

Juniper trees, grown from seeds brought from China

The thatched Senbutsu-jo serves as a meditation hall.

Karamon (Chinese gate)

Hatto

Former bath

The temple bell

Archery hall

The bridge over the White Heron pond

The Sanmon was built in 1783.

↑ The layout of Engaku-ji, a Zen Buddhist temple in Kamakura

Did You Know?

The sunrise seen from Mount Fuji is called *goraiko* - an overwhelming sight.

Mount Fuji towering over the town of Fujikawaguchiko ↑

3

MOUNT FUJI

富士山

⌂ Shizuoka & Yamanashi Prefectures 🚆 Fuji-san, Kawaguchi-ko, Gotenba, Mishima (Tokaido Shinkansen), Fujinomiya 🚌 Summer only, from all stations to the nearest 5th stage; also direct from Tokyo (Shinjuku station west side or Hamamatsu-cho) to Kawaguchi-ko, Gotenba, Lake Yamanaka Ⓦ fujisan-climb.jp

A true Japanese icon, the silhouette of Mount Fuji (Fujisan in Japanese) is famed the world over. At 12,390 ft (3,776 m), it is Japan's highest peak by far, its near-perfect cone floating lilacgray or snowcapped above hilltops and low cloud.

Dormant since 1707, the volcano first erupted 8,000–10,000 years ago, and its upper slopes are formed of loose volcanic ash, devoid of greenery. Until 150 years ago, Mount Fuji was considered so sacred that it was climbed only by pilgrims; women were not allowed until 1868. Today the hiking trails, which are divided into ten stages, are traversed by a host of climbers during the summer season. Climbers should be respectful of the environment, and are encouraged to provide donations to contribute to safety and conservation efforts. For those who don't want to make the climb, or for visitors during the closed season, there are magnificent views of the mountain throughout the Fuji Five Lakes area *(p168)*.

💬 INSIDER TIP
Tips for Walkers

You can only climb from July to mid-September. To catch the sunrise, start at the 5th stage in the afternoon, sleep in a hut at the 7th or 8th stage, and rise early to finish the climb. Watch out for altitude sickness above the 8th stage.

MOUNT FUJI IN ART

With its graceful, near symmetrical form, its changing appearance at different seasons and times of day, and its dominance over the landscape, Mount Fuji has always been a popular subject for artists. The sacred mountain features in various ukiyo-e prints *(p150)*, the most famous being Hokusai's *Thirty-Six Views of Mount Fuji* (1830–32), and *Fifty-Three Stages of the Tokaido* (1833–4), by Hiroshige. In other arts, Mount Fuji is echoed in decorative motifs, for instance on kimonos and in wood carvings.

→ Climbers around the torii (gate) at the mountain's summit

↑ The Shiraito waterfalls on the Fujinomiya trail, a five-hour trek from the 5th stage

FUJI FIVE LAKES

⌂ Yamanashi Prefecture 🚉🚌 3641-1 Funatsu, Fujikawaguchiko; www.japan.travel/en/destinations/tokai/yamanashi/fuji-five-lakes

Around the north of Mount Fuji is a lake region of lush countryside. The area is perfect for outdoor enthusiasts, full of cultural attractions, and offers spectacular views of the famous mountain that dominates the landscape.

↑ Brilliant flowers in bloom at Hananomiyako Koen park by Lake Yamanaka

① Lake Kawaguchi

⌂ Kawaguchiko 🌐 fujisan.ne.jp

Near the base of Mount Fuji is Lake Kawaguchi, a serene expanse of water surrounded by forests and hot springs. The eastern shore is the most developed, with bus and rail links to Tokyo and most of the area's hotels, restaurants, and shops. Head around the lake to the north, however, and you'll find some startlingly lovely views of the mountain, especially when the leaves turn red around October.

Highlights of the Lake Kawaguchi area include the quirky **Kawaguchiko Music Forest**, which focuses entirely on automatic instruments like music boxes and mechanical organs. A little farther along the lake's north shore is the Itchiko Kubota Museum, dedicated to the eponymous kimono artist. The building and grounds are full of fascinating artworks and breathtaking kimonos.

From the eastern shore of Lake Kawaguchi, the **Mount Kachi Kachi Ropeway** whisks you to the observation deck on Mount Tenjo in just a few minutes, offering uninterrupted views toward Mount Fuji. You can also hike up to the observation deck.

Kawaguchiko Music Forest

🌀🌀🍴🛍️📷 ⌂ 3077-20 Kawaguchi, Fujikawaguchiko 🕐 9:30am–5:30pm daily 🚪 Late Jan 🌐 fuji.kawaguchikomusicforest.jp

Itchiko Kubota Museum

🌀🍴📷 ⌂ 2255 Kawaguchi, Fujikawaguchiko-machi 🕐 Times vary, see website 🚪 Late Jan 🌐 itchiku-museum.com

Mount Kachi Kachi Ropeway

🌀🍴📷 ⌂ 1163 Azagawa, Fujikawaguchiko-machi 🕐 Mar–Nov: 9am–5pm daily; Dec–Feb: 9:30am–4:30pm daily 🌐 mtfujiropeway.jp

② Lake Yamanaka

🚌 🌐 yamanakako.gr.jp

The largest of the five lakes in the area, and the closest to

Mount Fuji, Lake Yamanaka is a little less developed and crowded than Lake Kawaguchi. It offers glorious views of Mount Fuji, and several relaxing *ryokan* (traditional Japanese inns) and *onsen* (hot springs), some boasting mountain views from their outdoor baths.

This area is a great base for outdoor activities such as hiking, cycling, and kayaking. As well as enjoying the area's abundant natural beauty – particularly along the less-developed north shore – you can see colorful seasonal flowers at the **Hananomiyako Koen** flower park. From the first green shoots of spring to summer's bold sunflowers, the blooms always complement Mount Fuji looming on the horizon.

Hananomiyako Koen

⊕ ⑨ ☺ ♨ ⌂ 1650 Yamanaka, Yamanakako-mura ⏰ Times vary, see website ⓦ hananomiyako kouen.jp

---

③
Oshino

📠 ℹ 239-3 Shibokusa, Oshino; www.oshino.jp

The small village of Oshino is dotted around eight clear, cool ponds – collectively known as the Oshino Hakkai – which are fed by snowmelt from Mount Fuji. Locals have developed a thriving tourist economy by carefully maintaining the traditional atmosphere and beautiful scenery, creating a spot that remains picturesque and pleasant despite the occasional summer crowds.

---

④
Chureito Pagoda

⌂ 3353-1 Arakura, Fuji-yoshida 🚉 Shimoyoshida, then a 20 minute walk ⏰ 24 hours daily

Part of Sengen Shrine, this five-story pagoda sits on a hillside with jaw-dropping views of Mount Fuji rising on the horizon. The Sengen shrine dates from the eighth century, but the pagoda itself was built in 1963 as a peace memorial. It's a long uphill walk from the nearest station to the pagoda, but the effort is worth it when the weather is fine and Mount Fuji is on full display. Even on cloudy days when the mountain may be obscured by cloud, the pagoda itself is beautiful and iconic landmark.

← Lake Kawaguchi in fall, with Mount Fuji shrouded in cloud on the horizon

---

EAT

Houtou Fudou
The best place to try Yamanashi Prefecture's regional dish, *houtou*, a hearty miso soup supposedly invented by 16th-century warlord Takeda Shingen to fortify his troops.

⌂ 707 Kawaguchi, Fujikawaguchiko-machi, Fujikawaguchiko ⓦ houtou-fudou.jp

¥ ¥ ¥

View of Mount Fuji from the hillside behind Chureito Pagoda

↑ Looking over Lake Chuzenji from the Futura-san Shrine

5

NIKKO

日光

🏠 Tochigi Prefecture 🚃 ℹ️ At Tobu Nikko Stn; www.nikko-travel.jp

Written with kanji characters that mean "sunlight," the town of Nikko has become a Japanese byword for splendor. In 766, the formidable Buddhist priest Shodo Shonin founded the first temple here. This was the first of many and Nikko became a renowned Buddhist-Shinto religious center, and the resting place of Tokugawa Ieyasu.

①

Takino-o Shrine

🏠 2310-1 Sannai 📞 (0288) 21-0765 🕐 24 hrs daily

This peaceful, rustic shrine, thought to be dedicated to a female deity, draws women and those looking for love. Toss a stone through the hole in the top of the torii and into the shrine grounds and your wish, they say, will come true.

②

Shinkyo Bridge

This red-lacquered wooden bridge, just to the left of the road bridge, arches over the Daiya River where, legend has it, Shodo Shonin crossed the water on the backs of two huge serpents. The original bridge, which was built in 1636 for the exclusive use of the shogun and imperial messengers, was destroyed by a flood. The current bridge dates from 1907.

③

Futara-san Shrine

🏠 2307 Sannai 🕐 8am–5pm daily (Nov–Mar: to 4pm) 🌐 futarasan.jp

Founded by Shodo Shonin in 782, this shrine is dedicated to the gods of the mountains Nantai (male), Nyotai (female), and Taro, their child. It is actually the main shrine of three; the other two are at Lake Chuzenji and on Mount Nantai. The bronze torii here has been designated as an Important Cultural Property. But the shrine's most interesting feature for visitors is a tall bronze lantern, nicknamed the "ghost lantern", which is said to take the shape of a monster at night. The gashes in the lamp are from the sword of a terrified samurai who attacked it when the flame started to flicker in a peculiar way. A vermilion fence now protects the lantern from attack.

④

Rinno-ji

🏠 2300 Sannai 🕐 8am–5pm daily

The first temple in Nikko, founded by Buddhist priest Shodo Shonin in 766, Rinno-ji was originally called Shihonryu-ji. When it became a Tendai-sect temple in the 17th century, it was renamed. Its Sanbutsu-do (Three Buddha Hall) is the largest hall at Nikko. The three gilt images – of Amida Buddha, Senju (thousand-armed) Kannon, and Bato (horse-headed) Kannon – enshrined in the hall correspond to the three mountain deities enshrined at Futara-san Shrine. Beyond the hall, the nine-ringed bronze pillar, Sorinto, contains 1,000 volumes of sutras (Buddhist scriptures) and is a symbol of world peace.

The temple's beautiful Treasure Hall (Homotsuden) houses a large and fascinating array of temple treasures, mainly dating from the Edo period. Behind it is the Shoyoen, a lovely Edo-style 19th-century stroll garden that has been carefully landscaped so that it is at its best for every season. The enchanting path through the garden meanders around a large pond, over stone bridges, and past mossy stone lanterns.

←

An imposing statue of Shodo Shonin found near Rinno-ji

⑤
Kanman-ga-Fuchi Abyss

🚌 Nishisando

Lava flows from an old eruption of Mount Nantai combine with the limpid waters of the Daiya River to make these unusual scenic pools. It is not hard to see why the Abyss is a sacred spot to Buddhism. About 70 stone statues of Jizo, the bodhisattva of children, line the path by the river. They are known as phantom statues because their numbers appear to change every time you look.

---

⑥
Nikko Botanical Gardens

🏠 1842 Hanaishicho
📞 (0288) 54-0206
🚌 Nikko Shokubutsuen
🕘 9am–4:30pm Tue–Sun
🔒 Dec 1–Apr 14

Some 3,000 varieties of plants and flowers from Japan and around the world can be seen at these gardens, a branch of the Koishikawa Botanical Gardens of the University of Tokyo. Flora from Nikko National Park are showcased. April to July, when skunk cabbages and irises bloom, is a lovely time to visit.

⑦
Urushi Museum

🏠 2829-1 Tokorono
📞 (0288) 53-6807
🚌 Marumi 🕘 Mar 16–Nov 11: Sat, Sun, Mon

This small museum showcases lacquerware arts – *urushi* means lacquer. Used in Japan for over 5,000 years, lacquer has reached the height of refinement only in the past 1,000 years. The museum's collection also includes decorative wares from China, India, and Egypt.

EAT

Nikko Yuba Zen
This minimalist restaurant, which seats just ten people, offers a modern twist on Nikko's famous *yuba* dish (tofu skins).

🏠 1007 Kamihatsuishimachi
🔒 Tue 🌐 nikkoyuba makizen.gorp.jp

¥ ¥ ¥

TOSHO-GU SHRINE

東照宮

🏯 2301 Sannai ⏰ 8am-5pm daily (Nov-Mar: to 4pm)
🌐 toshogu.jp

Tokugawa Iemitsu set out to dazzle with this mausoleum-shrine for his grandfather Ieyasu. For two years some 15,000 artisans from all over Japan worked, building, carving, gilting, painting, and lacquering, to create this flowery, gorgeous Momoyama-style complex.

Although designated a Shinto shrine in the Meiji period, Tosho-gu retains many of its original Buddhist elements, including the sutra library, which chronicles the temple's history, the Niomon Gate, and an unusual pagoda with a suspended pillar. The famed *sugi-namiki* (Japanese cedar avenue) leading to the shrine was planted by a 17th-century lord, in lieu of a more opulent offering. The shrine is undergoing major renovation work, which is scheduled to be completed in 2024, though most of it is still open to visitors. Don't miss the Tokugawa armor in the Treasure Hall or the painted doors in the Museum of Art.

→

The embellished structures making up the Tosho-gu Shrine complex

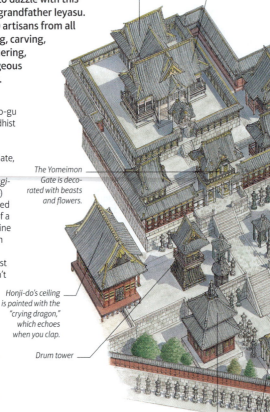

Honden (main hall)

Haiden (worship hall)

The Yomeimon Gate is decorated with beasts and flowers.

Honji-do's ceiling is painted with the "crying dragon," which echoes when you clap.

Drum tower

The Rinzo contains a sutra library of Buddhist scriptures set within a revolving structure.

The sacred fountain is covered with an ornate Chinese-style roof. The granite basin (1618) is used for ritual purification.

TOKUGAWA IEYASU

Ieyasu (1543–1616) was a wily strategist and master politician who founded the Tokugawa dynasty that would rule Japan for over 250 years. Born the son of a minor lord, he spent his life accumulating power, before becoming shogun in 1603. He built his capital in the swampy village of Edo (now Tokyo), and his rule saw the start of the flowering of Edo culture. After his death, he was enshrined and given his posthumous name: Tosho-Daigongen, "the great incarnation illuminating the East".

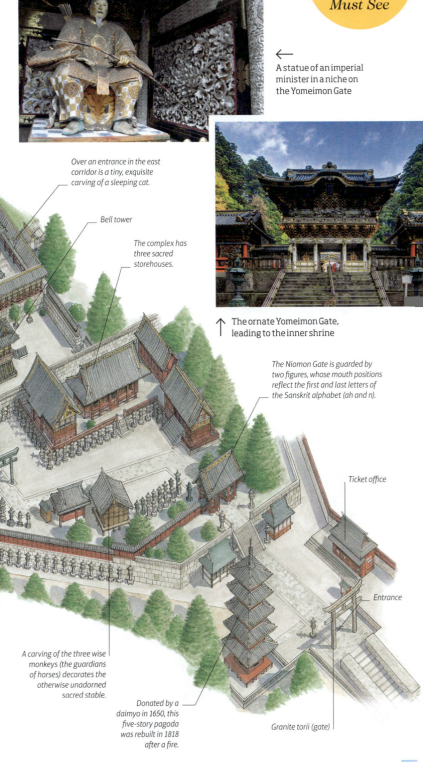

← A statue of an imperial minister in a niche on the Yomeimon Gate

Over an entrance in the east corridor is a tiny, exquisite carving of a sleeping cat.

Bell tower

The complex has three sacred storehouses.

↑ The ornate Yomeimon Gate, leading to the inner shrine

The Niomon Gate is guarded by two figures, whose mouth positions reflect the first and last letters of the Sanskrit alphabet (ah and n).

Ticket office

Entrance

A carving of the three wise monkeys (the guardians of horses) decorates the otherwise unadorned sacred stable.

Donated by a daimyo in 1650, this five-story pagoda was rebuilt in 1818 after a fire.

Granite torii (gate)

⑨ 🗺️

TAIYUIN-BYO SHRINE

大猷院廟

🏠 2300 Sannai 📞 (0288) 53-1567 🕐 8am–5pm daily (Nov–Mar: to 4pm)

If Tosho-gu is splendid, Taiyuin-byo is sublime. It was built modestly so that it would not eclipse Tosho-gu, a sign of deep respect to Tokugawa Ieyasu. Despite this restraint, it is still an ornate tomb reflecting the power of the imperial family.

Completed in 1653, Taiyuin-byo is the mausoleum of Tokugawa Iemitsu (1604–51), the powerful third Tokugawa shogun and grandson of Ieyasu, who closed Japan to foreign commerce and isolated it from the world for over 200 years. Tayuin is his posthumous Buddhist name. As with Tosho-gu, Taiyuin-byo has retained many of its Buddhist elements, despite being reconsecrated as a Shinto shrine in the Meiji period. Set in a grove of Japanese cedars, it has a number of ornate gates ascending to the Haiden (worship hall), where you can admire the grand interior's coffered ceilings and carvings. The Honden (main hall) behind this is usually closed to the public. The shogun's ashes are entombed beyond the sixth and final gate.

The Honden holds a gilded Buddhist altar with a wooden statue of Iemitsu.

Decorated with carvings of dragons, the Haiden also has some famous 17th-century lion paintings.

Did You Know?

To stop him seizing power, Iemitsu forced his brother Tadanaga to commit seppuku.

1 The drum and bell towers are no longer used, but the drum signifies positivity/birth, while the bell denotes negativity/death.

2 As well as being inlaid with peonies, the Yashamon Gate is also ornamented with four statues of Yasha, a fierce guardian spirit.

3 Marking the main entrance to the shrine, a powerful red-faced Nio warrior god stands guard on either side of the Niomon Gate, frightening away evil spirits.

Entrance

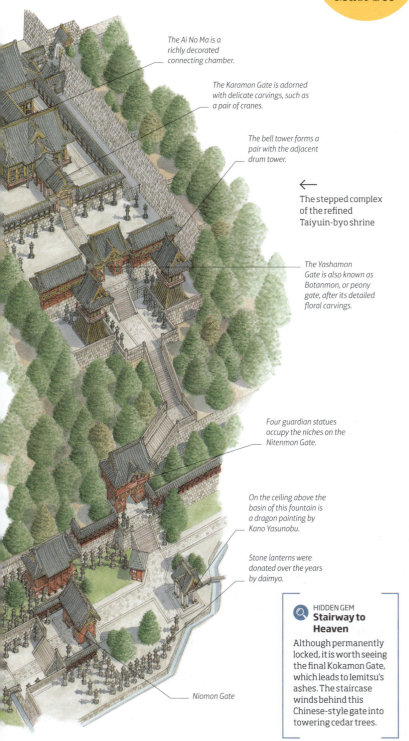

The Ai No Ma is a richly decorated connecting chamber.

The Karamon Gate is adorned with delicate carvings, such as a pair of cranes.

The bell tower forms a pair with the adjacent drum tower.

←

The stepped complex of the refined Taiyuin-byo shrine

The Yashamon Gate is also known as Botanmon, or peony gate, after its detailed floral carvings.

Four guardian statues occupy the niches on the Nitenmon Gate.

On the ceiling above the basin of this fountain is a dragon painting by Kano Yasunobu.

Stone lanterns were donated over the years by daimyo.

Niomon Gate

> ### HIDDEN GEM
> **Stairway to Heaven**
>
> Although permanently locked, it is worth seeing the final Kokamon Gate, which leads to Iemitsu's ashes. The staircase winds behind this Chinese-style gate into towering cedar trees.

EXPERIENCE MORE

6

Narita
成田

⊠🏠🚌 ℹ 839 Hanazakicho, Narita, Chiba Prefecture; www.nrtk.jp

The city of Narita is worlds away from its nearby bustling airport, with Omotesando Dori looking more like the streets of Kyoto than something from the Tokyo Metropolitan area. The town's main attraction is Narita-san Shinsho-ji, an interesting Esoteric Shingon-sect temple founded in 940 and dedicated to Fudo Myo-o, Deity of Immovable Wisdom. Several times daily, the priests burn wooden sticks to symbolize the extinguishing of earthly passions. The streets are full of traditional shops for the 12 million temple visitors a year.

Did You Know?

Narita is famous for its eel restaurants, which once served Edo lords en route to Tokyo.

Near Narita are over 1,000 ancient burial mounds (*kofun*); the best are in the open-air museum, **Boso no Mura**. One stop from Narita on the Keisei Line express service, the **National Museum of Japanese History** offers a good survey of Japan.

Boso no Mura

🏠 1028 Ryukakuji, Sakae, Inba ℂ (0476) 95-3333 🕘 9am–4:30pm Tue–Sun

National Museum of Japanese History

 🏠 117 Jonaicho, Sakura ℂ (043) 486-0123 🕘 Mar–Sep: 9:30am–5pm Tue–Sun (Oct–Feb: to 4:30pm)

7

Kawagoe
川越

🏠🚌 ℹ 24-9 Wakitamachi, Kawagoe, Saitama Prefecture; www.koedo.or.jp

Nicknamed "Little Edo," Kawagoe preserves the atmosphere of 19th-century Edo (the original name for Tokyo) because of its *kura* buildings. These clay-walled structures have double doors, and heavy shutters. About 30 *kura* remain and are a ten-minute walk north of Hon-Kawagoe station. Nearby, Toki-no-kane wooden bell tower was built in 1624 to tell the time and warn of fires. East of the *kura* streets is Kita-in, a Tendai-sect temple which includes the only extant rooms from Edo Castle.

At one time, Kawagoe possessed its own castle, which was the dominant structure in the town. Part of that castle remains in the shape of **Honmaru Goten**, the former residence of the lord, with many commodious rooms.

Honmaru Goten

 🏠 2-13-1 Kurawa-machi ℂ (049) 224-6015 🕘 9am–5pm Tue–Sun

8

Hakone
箱根

🏠🚌 ℹ 706-35 Yumoto, Hakone, Kanagawa Prefecture; www.hakone.or.jp

Hakone is a hilly hot-spring town, with scattered cultural and natural attractions. The Hakone area extends

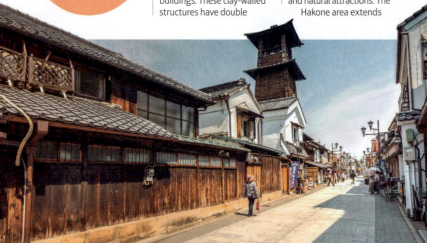

↑ Wandering past steaming sulphur vents in Owakudani valley, Hakone

across the collapsed remains of a huge volcano, which was active until 3,000–4,000 years ago, leaving a legacy today of hot springs and steam vents.

Although Hakone can be visited as a long day trip from Tokyo, it is worth an overnight stay. Two- or three-day public-transportation passes are available on the Odakyu line from Shinjuku, Tokyo. A convenient circuit of the main sights starts from the *onsen* town of Hakone-Yumoto, taking the Tozan switchback train up the hillside to **Hakone Open-Air Museum**, with its modern sculptures. Continue via funicular to **Hakone Museum of Art**, which has an excellent Japanese ceramic collection and garden. Via the funicular and then a ropeway over the crest of the hill is the fascinating Owaku-dani ("valley of great boiling"), an area of sulfurous steam vents. This is an active volcanic zone, so sometimes the ropeway or sections of this area are closed to visitors for safety reasons. The ropeway continues to Lake Ashi, where replicas of historical Western-style boats

←

Old-fashioned street in Kawagoe, with *kura* buildings and a wooden clock tower

run to Hakone-machi and Moto-Hakone. In clear weather there are stunning views of Mount Fuji. At Hakone-machi is an interesting reconstruction of the **Sekisho Barrier Gate**, a checkpoint that used to control passage on the Edo-period Tokaido road between Tokyo and Kyoto.

From Hakone-machi it is a short walk to Moto-Hakone. Located on a hilltop overlooking Lake Ashi, **Narukawa Art Museum** exhibits 1,500 artworks by modern Japanese masters, and has spectacular views of the surrounding mountains. Over a pass beyond Moto-Hakone is the Amazake-chaya teahouse, and Hatajuku village, known for *yosegi-zaiku*, a form of decorative marquetry.

Hakone Open-Air Museum
 1121 Ninotaira
🕘 9am–5pm daily
🌐 hakone-oam.or.jp

Hakone Museum of Art
📍 1300 Gora 📞 (0460) 82-2623 🕘 9am–4:30pm Fri–Wed (Dec–Mar: to 5pm)

Sekisho Barrier Gate
🕘 9am–5pm daily (Dec–Feb: to 4:30pm) 🌐 hakone sekisyo.jp

Narukawa Art Museum
📍 570 Motohakone
🕘 9am–5pm daily
🌐 narukawamuseum.co.jp

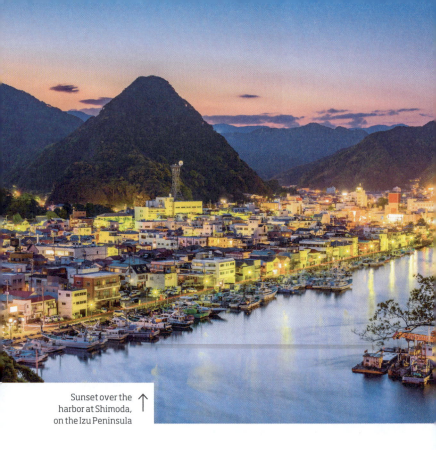

Sunset over the harbor at Shimoda, on the Izu Peninsula ↑

 9

Izu Peninsula
伊豆半島

🚆🚌 **ℹ** Atami, Ito, and Shuzenji Stations; www.exploreshizuoka.com

A hilly peninsula with a benign climate, Izu is popular for its many hot springs. A place of exile during the Middle Ages, in the early 1600s it was home to shipwrecked sailor William Adams, the Englishman whose story was the basis of the James Clavell novel *Shogun* (1975).

Izu's east coast is quite developed, but the west has charming coves and fishing villages, such as Toi and Heda, offering delicious long-legged crabs and other seafood. The center is also relatively unspoiled, with wooded mountains and rustic hot springs. The whole region has become a popular area for cycling holidays, with its dynamic landscapes, and the many *onsens* (hot springs) making a great way to relax at the end of a day of cycling.

 10

Shizuoka
静岡

🚆🚌 **ℹ** 49-1 Kuroganecho, Aoi, Shizuoka Prefecture; www.visit-shizuoka.com

Settlement in this area dates back to 200 AD. Once a stop on the old Tokaido road (an important travel route in Edo-era Japan), and the retirement home of Tokugawa Ieyasu (*p54*), Shizuoka is today a sprawling urban center, the city in Japan at greatest risk of a major earthquake – and probably the only place that is fully prepared.

The **Toro ruins** near the port have reconstructions of ancient buildings and an excellent museum. The view from Nihondaira plateau, in the east of the city, to Mount Fuji and Izu is superb. Nearby, the Oigawa steam railroad takes you right into the untamed Minami Alps mountain range.

Toro ruins

⊘ 🚆 5-10-5 Toro 📞 (054) 285-0476 🕐 9am–4:30pm Tue–Sun

 11

Katsunuma

🚆🚌 **ℹ** 1-2-14 Marunouchi, Kofu, Yamanashi Prefecture; www.yamanashi-kankou.jp

The town of Katsunuma may only be a 90-minute train ride

 INSIDER TIP
Chichibu Whiskey

Ichiro's Malt CHICHIBU is regularly ranked one of the best whiskeys in the world. The distillery was founded in Chichibu city in 2008.

12

Chichibu-Tama-Kai National Park
秩父多摩甲斐国立公園

 Several Prefectures
Seibu-Chichibu, Chichibu, Okutama, Mitake
Seibu-Chichibu Stn; www.env.go.jp

This vast national park is spread across a region of low mountains, stretching from the narrow valleys of Okutama in the south to Chichibu city in the north. The two parts of the park are separated by mountains, crossed only by a few hiking trails. Within the park, railroads reach a few spots, but travel is mostly by bus. A silk-producing area until the early 1900s, Chichibu is now known for a pilgrim route linking 34 Kannon temples. Elsewhere in the area, Mount Mitake has a mountaintop shrine village, and the **Nippara Caves** are worth visiting.

Nippara Caves

Nippara, Okutama
(0428) 83-2099 8am–5pm daily

13

Suntory Hakushu Distillery

2913-1 Hakushucho Torihara, Hokuto, Yamanashi Prefecture
Times vary, see website
suntory.com

Anyone interested in good whiskey should make sure to add Hakushu Distillery in Yamanashi Prefecture to their Japan itinerary. Hakushu is situated on the slopes of Mount Kaikoma, completely surrounded by forest, which creates a uniquely peaceful atmosphere. At 2,296 ft (700 m) above sea level, this is one of the highest distilleries in the world, and the altitude means that the boiling temperature is lower. This, in combination with the soft local mountain water, produces one of Japan's finest whiskeys. The high elevation also has an impact on the aging process, meaning that the whiskey matures more slowly. At the small, but excellent, museum you can learn about the history of Japanese whiskey-making, while the worthwhile tour of the distillery finishes with a tutorial on how to make the perfect highball.

TOP 3 **THEME PARKS BEYOND TOKYO**

Sanrio Puroland
1-31 Ochiai, Tama, Tokyo Prefecture puroland.jp
Hello Kitty fans will love this theme park full of musicals, rides, restaurants, and cute Sanrio characters.

Tokyo Disney Resort®
1-1 Maihama, Urayasu, Chiba Prefecture tokyodisneyresort.jp
Made of two parks (Disneyland® and DisneySea®) this resort is one of the top five most-visited theme parks in the world.

Fuji-Q Highland
5-6-1 Shinnishihara, Fujiyoshida, Yamanashi Prefecture fujiq.jp
Best known for its exhilarating roller-coasters, haunted houses, and anime-themed attractions.

away from Tokyo, but with its lush green hills and towering mountains, it feels a million miles away from the bustle of the city.

Grape-growing here dates back to the 17th century and the area is now the heart of Japan's wine industry, its surrounding hills striped with rows of grapevines and dotted with wineries. Home to the country's unique *koshu* grape, Katsunuma boasts 31 wineries. Here, amidst the stunning scenery visitors can explore Japan's viticultural heritage. The enormous wine complex, **Budo no Oka**, with its hotel, vineyard, *onsen*, restaurants, tasting cave, and stunning views, combines the best of the area.

Budo no Oka

 5093 Katsunumacho Hishiyama, Koshu budounooka.com

A LONG WALK
ENOSHIMA

Distance 3 miles (5 km) **Walking time** 60 minutes
Terrain This walk includes a number of steep hills,
but there are escalators available for a small fee
Nearest station Katase-Enoshima

Southwest of Kamakura (p160), the island of Enoshima
juts up from the water of Sagami Bay, connected to the
mainland by bridge. For centuries, it has been a place of
pilgrimage associated with the goddess Benten, who is
believed to have created Enoshima before subduing a
disruptive, five-headed dragon. Though it may be small,
the island is full of interesting spots to explore: beautiful
shrines, a surprisingly stylish lighthouse, an English
garden, and ancient caves. The walk around the island
is also punctuated by stunning vistas out over the ocean,
with Mount Fuji visible to the west on a clear day. Adding to
Enoshima's charm are the narrow, winding paths flanked
by traditional Japanese houses, stacked pell-mell along
the cliffs, as well as the quirky escalators built to carry
visitors up some of the hills. A number of independent
cafés and traditional restaurants dot the island,
and adventurous foodies can visit ice cream
vendors selling bizarre flavors such
as *shirasu*, a local delicacy
comprising thousands of
tiny translucent white fish.

Did You Know?

The Enopass grants
admission to the
island's main sights,
use of escalators, and
shop discounts.

*The Samuel Cocking
Gardens offer a
beautiful array of
both Japanese and
European flowers.*

Hetsunomiya Shrine
Hoanden
Samuel Cocking Gardens
Yasaka Shrine
Enoshima Sea Candle
Yama-Futatsu
Okutsumiya Shrine
Torii Gate
Enoshima Iwaya Caves
FINISH
Bell of the Dragon's Love
Enoshima Daishi

*The **Iwaya Caves** have
been a site of pilgrimage
for Benten worshippers for
over 1500 years. The caves
are dotted with statues
donated by pilgrims over
the centuries.*

*Take a detour to the **Bell
of the Dragon's Love**,
which is meant to bring
good fortune to couples
who ring the bell and
attach a padlock to the
nearby fence.*

*In the middle of the
garden stands the
towering **Enoshima
Sea Candle**. From
this hyper modern
tower's observation
deck, visitors can see
across Enoshima
and Sagami Bay to
the Izu Peninsula in
the southwest, and
Mount Fuji to the west.*

BEYOND TOKYO
Tokyo
Enoshima

Locator Map
For more detail see p156

0 meters 200
0 yards 200
N

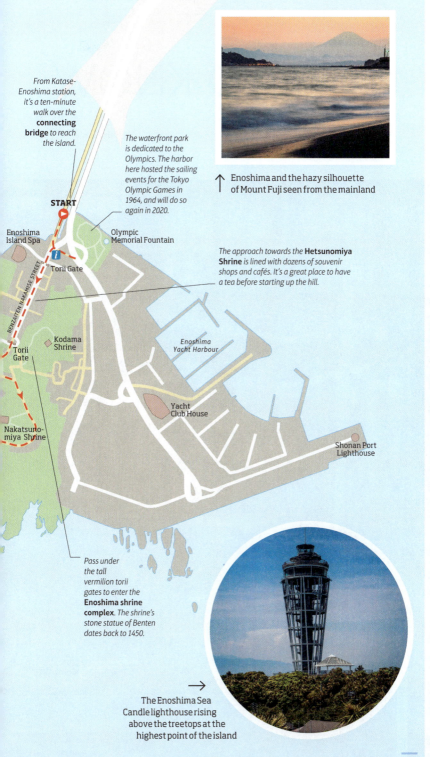

From Katase-Enoshima station, it's a ten-minute walk over the **connecting bridge** to reach the island.

The waterfront park is dedicated to the Olympics. The harbor here hosted the sailing events for the Tokyo Olympic Games in 1964, and will do so again in 2020.

↑ Enoshima and the hazy silhouette of Mount Fuji seen from the mainland

START

Enoshima Island Spa

ⓘ

Torii Gate

BENZAITEN NAKAMISE STREET

Olympic Memorial Fountain

The approach towards the **Hetsunomiya Shrine** is lined with dozens of souvenir shops and cafés. It's a great place to have a tea before starting up the hill.

Kodama Shrine

Torii Gate

Enoshima Yacht Harbour

Yacht Club House

Nakatsuno-miya Shrine

Shonan Port Lighthouse

Pass under the tall vermilion torii gates to enter the **Enoshima shrine complex**. The shrine's stone statue of Benten dates back to 1450.

→
The Enoshima Sea Candle lighthouse rising above the treetops at the highest point of the island

NEED TO KNOW

Cycling over a railroad crossing

BEFORE YOU GO

Forward planning is essential for any successful trip. Prepare yourself for any eventuality by brushing up on the following points before you set off.

AT A GLANCE

CURRENCY
Japanese Yen (¥)

AVERAGE DAILY SPEND

SAVE	SPEND	SPLURGE
¥10,000	¥20,000	¥40,000

BOTTLED WATER	COFFEE	BEER	DINNER FOR TWO
¥100	¥300	¥400	¥5,000

ESSENTIAL PHRASES

Hello	Konnichiwa
Goodbye	Sayonara
Please	Onegaishimasu
Thank you	Arigato Gozaimasu
Do you speak English?	Eigo o Hanasemasuka?
I don't understand	Wakarimasen

ELECTRICITY SUPPLY

Power sockets are type A and B. Standard voltage is 100v and the frequency is 50 Hz (east) and 60 Hz (west).

Passports and Visas

For a stay of up to three months for the purpose of tourism, EU nationals and citizens of the US, Canada, Australia, New Zealand and many other countries, do not need a visa. Citizens of some countries, including the UK and parts of the EU, may extend this stay by another 90 days at immigration offices in Japan (at least 10 days before the expiration date).

Visa Information
🅦 mofa.go.jp/j_info/visit/visa

Travel Safety Advice

Visitors can get travel safety information from the **US State Department** and **UK Foreign and Commonwealth Office**.

Each year, Japan experiences over 1,000 earthquakes large enough to be felt, but most are nothing to worry about. The Tokyo Government has issued a useful **Earthquake Survival Manual** with simple safety guidelines to follow in the event of stronger tremors.

US
🅦 travel.state.gov
UK
🅦 gov.uk/foreign-travel-advice
Earthquake Survival Manual
🅦 metro.tokyo.jp/english/guide/bosai/index.html

Climate

During spring (April–May) and fall (October–November), the weather is usually mild and pleasant. The rainy season lasts from early June to mid–July, while typhoon season peaks in August and September. July and August tend to be incredibly hot and humid, and winter can bring temperatures low enough for snow in the regions outside the Tokyo metropolitan area.

Customs Information

An individual is permitted to carry the following within Japan for personal use:
Tobacco products 400 cigarettes, 100 cigars, or 500g of smoking tobacco.

Alcohol Three 760-ml-bottles of alcoholic beverages.

Cash If you plan to enter Japan with ¥1 million or more in cash, you must declare it upon arrival.

Medicines Some over-the-counter medicines, such as those for sinus problems, and pain-killers containing codeine, are prohibited. Prescription drugs are also limited.

Insurance

It is wise to take out an insurance policy covering theft, loss of belongings, medical problems, cancellations, and delays. It is important to confirm that your policy covers medical costs since these can be extremely high in Japan.

Language

Tokyo is well signposted in English, and it is not hard for visitors to find their way around. Many, especially younger, Japanese people do speak at least a little English, but may use Japanese pronunciation – for example taxi becomes *takushi*, and hotel is *hoteru*.

Vaccinations

No inoculations are needed for Japan.

Booking Accommodations

As well as Western-style hotels, Tokyo offers a few idiosyncratic options. *Ryokans* are traditional inns which may have an on-site *onsen* (hot spring), and serve breakfast and dinner. At the opposite end of the scale, capsule hotels are highly modern, and offer inexpensive sleeping pods. These make for convenient short stays, but aren't suited to visitors who want space to unpack their suitcase.

For help with booking accommodations, visit the **Japan National Tourism Organization**.
Japan National Tourism Organization
w jnto.go.jp/ja-search/eng/index.php

Money

Although ATMs are very common in Tokyo, some do not accept foreign credit or debit cards, and some may not operate 24/7, so it is still worth carrying around some cash at all times. Cards can be used at major stations to buy JR train tickets and are accepted by most taxis.

Travelers with Specific Needs

The visually impaired are well provided for in Tokyo, but people in wheelchairs occasionally have issues at small stations without elevators, and pedestrian over- and underpasses, despite a 2008 law requiring barrier-free access. **Accessible Tokyo** provides information about disabled access and facilities in the capital, as well as Yokohama and Kamakura.
Accessible Tokyo
w accessible.jp.org

Closures

Monday Museums, art galleries, and many tourist attractions close for the day; when Monday is a bank holiday, they often close on Tuesday instead.

Weekends Banks, post offices, and offices are closed. Department stores may have reduced opening hours on Sunday.

Public holidays Many attractions are closed, as well as banks, post offices, and offices.

PUBLIC HOLIDAYS	
Jan 1	New Year's Day
2nd Mon, Jan	Coming of Age Day
Feb 11	National Foundation Day
Feb 23	Emperor's Birthday
Mar 20/21	Vernal (Spring) Equinox
Apr 29	Showa Day
May 3	Constitution Memorial Day
May 4	Greenery Day
May 5	Children's Day
3rd Mon, Jul	Marine Day
Aug 11	Mountain Day
3rd Mon, Sep	Respect for the Aged Day
Sep 22/23	Autumnal Equinox
2nd Mon, Oct	Health and Sports Day
Nov 3	Culture Day
Nov 23	Labor Thanksgiving Day

GETTING AROUND

Discover how to navigate with ease around one of the most densely packed and complex, yet fascinating megacities in the world.

AT A GLANCE

PUBLIC TRANSPORTATION

SUBWAY

¥170

A single subway journey

TRAIN (JR)

¥140

A single train (JR) journey

BUS

¥210

A single bus journey

TOP TIP

Buy a reloadable Suica or Pasmo card to save time on Tokyo transportation.

TRAVEL ETIQUETTE

Bags
Hold your backpack or luggage in front of you to make space for others.

Talking
Talking loudly, especially on a cell phone, is considered disrespectful toward other passengers.

Food
Eating is deemed bad manners, except on long-distance journeys.

Lining Up
When waiting for a train or bus, line up neatly. Let other people off the train first.

Disembarking
To get off a crowded train, gently push through and call out "*Orimasu*" ("I'm getting off") so people know to make way.

Arriving by Air

The main international gateways to Tokyo are **Narita International Airport** and **Haneda Airport**. Narita is some distance away from the city center, but despite its inconvenient location, it is well connected with a multitude of travel options, including two express trains into Tokyo. Haneda, located on the southern edge of the city only 14 km (8.6 miles) from Tokyo Station, is a much smaller airport, but is further expanding its international flight capacity and can be easily reached by local train or monorail.

Narita International Airport
ⓦ narita-airport.jp
Haneda Airport
ⓦ haneda-airport.jp/inter

Train Travel

Tokyo's railroad system is the most extensive and busiest in the world, but it is also extremely clean, efficient, safe, and famously punctual, making navigating this giant labyrinth more a pleasure than a nightmare. Some of the city's huge stations can be daunting, but the system is very well organized, with color-coded train lines and maps, directional arrows, and bilingual signs. Trains run from around 5am to just after midnight daily. Avoid rush hour (8–9am and 6–8pm) if possible, especially if you are carrying luggage or traveling with small children.

Train Lines

There are several private railroad companies running in Tokyo, as well as an excellent subway system run by the Tokyo Metro & Toei Subway companies. Despite the multitude of operators, transferring between lines is rarely troublesome due to good signage and a well coordinated, digitized ticketing system. Trains running on the same lines are usually divided into *tokkyu* ("limited express"), *kyuko* ("express"), *kaisoku* ("rapid"), and *futsu* ("local"), so it is important to check the type of train before boarding as express trains skip many smaller local stations.

For those wanting to head for other destinations across the country, Tokyo Station is the

GETTING TO AND FROM THE AIRPORT

Airport	Destination	Bus	Taxi	Train	Express
Narita	Tokyo Station	¥1,000	¥20,000	¥1,200	¥3,020
		(90 mins)	(70 mins)	(90 mins)	(55 mins)
	Shinjuku Station	¥3,100	¥22,000	¥1,230	¥3,190
		(90 mins)	(75 mins)	(100 mins)	(80 mins)
	Shibuya Station	¥3,100	¥22,000	¥1,260	¥3,190
		(90 mins)	(75 mins)	(115 mins	(75 mins)
	Nippori Station				¥2,470
					(35 mins)
Haneda	Tokyo Station	¥930	¥6,720	¥580	
		(55 mins)	(25 mins)	(35 mins)	
	Shinjuku Station	¥1,230	¥8,030	¥610	
		(30 mins)	(35 mins)	(50 mins)	
	Shibuya Station	¥1,030	¥7,420	¥580	
		(50 mins)	(30 mins)	(45 mins)	

major departure point and terminus for the *shinkansen*, although those traveling on the Tokaido Line to western destinations, including Kyoto and Hiroshima, can also board the bullet train at Shinagawa Station. Tickets and seat reservations for the bullet train can be bought at most JR stations in Tokyo. Seat reservations, which are charged at a small extra fee, are recommended for long-distance trips, especially during public holidays when unreserved cars can become extremely crowded.

Passes

The **Japan Rail Pass** (JR Pass) is recommended for those planning to travel extensively through-out Japan, but a number of JR regional rail passes are also available that cover specific areas closer to Tokyo. For those not traveling too far from the capital, there is the **JR TOKYO Wide Pass** which covers popular sites in the region, including Lake Kawaguchi, Nikko, and the Izu Peninsula.

Japan Rail Pass
Ⓦ jreast.co.jp/e/pass/index.html
JR TOKYO Wide Pass
Ⓦ jreast.co.jp/e/tokyowidepass

Long-Distance Bus Travel

The efficiency and extent of the rail network mean that few visitors to Tokyo use long-distance coaches to travel to and from the city, but Japan's highway bus network is comprehensive, and for those without a JR Pass, a bus is a much cheaper option than the bullet train. Those traveling long distances can also usually get an overnight bus.

Multiple companies run long-distance services from the capital, so travelers are able to plan their journey by convenience of departure point and destination. Coaches depart from many locations around the city – usually near major train stations – but the epicenter of bus travel in Tokyo is the modern, multi-story **Shinjuku Expressway Bus Terminal** (*Busuta Shinjuku* in Japanese). This is located across the road from Shinjuku Station's South Exit, and is directly connected to the New South Gate. The fourth floor is for highway bus departures and the third floor is for arrivals.

Tokyo Station is the other major junction for buses coming to and from the city, and the **Tokyo Expressway Bus Terminal** is situated on the east side of the station. Departures and arrivals are separated, with the long-distance boarding dock and ticketing window located just in front of the station's Yaesu South Exit gate, while arriving coaches pull in by the Nihonbashi Exit.

Shinjuku Expressway Bus Terminal
Ⓦ shinjuku-busterminal.co.jp
Tokyo Expressway Bus Terminal
Ⓦ tokyo-busterminal.tokyo

Public Transportation

Equipped to handle a daytime population that swells to well over 10 million every weekday, Tokyo's public transportation system is remarkably diverse and reliable.

Besides using the very efficient subway system, visitors can explore the city by bus, overground train (notably JR's Yamanote and Chuo lines, and the private railroad lines), tram, monorail, boat, taxi, bicycle, and even rickshaw. Maps are available at tourist information centers and many train stations throughout the city.

Tickets

Basic fare tickets for short distances are bought from ticket machines at stations, and virtually all of these will have an English-translation button. Most stations have maps in English, indicating the fares to different destinations. If in doubt about the cost of a trip, simply buy a cheap ticket and pay any excess at the destination using the fare adjustment machine near the exit barrier. This machine will supply you with a new ticket. If there is no such machine, station staff will work out the additional charge; you will not be penalized for having the wrong-value ticket.

In Tokyo there are a wide variety of single or multi-day passes available for the different transport operators, but they are not usually worth the inconvenience of being limited to certain lines. The **Tokyo 1-Day Ticket** (known as "*Free Kippu*" in Japanese) is probably the most flexible pass option, as it allows 24 hours of unlimited travel within Tokyo's 23 wards on most of the JR, subway, bus, and streetcar lines (excluding all private railroad lines). This pass can be purchased at any JR station for ¥1,590 (children ¥800).

For those planning on making use of Tokyo's extensive subway system, it is worth considering a **Chika Toku** pass, which allows unlimited subway travel for either 24, 48 or 72 hours, and can also be used to obtain various discounts at certain attractions, restaurants, and shops.

Most travelers opt to buy either a **Suica**, or **Pasmo** IC card. These convenient and flexible interoperable smart cards can be used on virtually all forms of public transportation in Tokyo and surrounding areas. Suica cards can be purchased at JR train stations, either over the counter or from vending machines. Pasmo cards can be bought at stations on the subway system or at one of Tokyo's numerous private railroad line stations. There is no discernible difference between the two types of cards, which can be used interchangeably on the network and both cost ¥1,000. This price includes a ¥500 deposit which is refunded when the card is returned, along with any unused funds – although with Suica a commission fee of ¥220 is also deducted

from the remaining balance. Both cards can also be used for making purchases at an increasing number of shops, especially convenience stores, as well as at vending machines, station lockers and numerous other locations – just look for a card reader with the Suica or Pasmo mark.

Tokyo 1-Day Ticket
🅦 jreast.co.jp/e/pass/tokyo_free.html

Chika Toku
🅦 chikatoku.enjoytokyo.jp

Suica
🅦 jreast.co.jp/e/pass/suica.html

Pasmo
🅦 pasmo.co.jp

Subway

Tokyo's subway network is extensive and consists of the Tokyo Metro (nine lines) and Toei Subway (four lines) systems. Tokyo Metro and Toei Subway have different symbols (a white "M" on a blue background and a green fan-shaped symbol respectively), but they share the same subway sign (a blue train on its track), which is usually prominent at the street-level entrance to the subway. Besides being color-coded, each subway line is designated a letter (G for the Ginza Line, for example), and each station is assigned a number. Hence, Shibuya, the western terminal of the Ginza Line, is G-01.

Color-coded subway maps in English are available at all major train and metro stations, many hotels, and tourist information centers.

Local Buses

Several bus companies connect many parts of Tokyo. This method of travel is particularly good for local hot spots that may not be on the main tourist paths, and therefore not easily reached by subway or train – however, the lack of English signage can pose more of a difficulty.

Bus stands (*basu noriba*) are usually located in front of major train stations. Buses in central Tokyo have a flat-fare system and charge ¥210 (¥110 for children). Unlike in many other parts of Japan, you board the bus by the front door, place your fare in the box beside the driver or touch your prepaid Suica or Pasmo card on the sensor, and exit from the door in the middle of the bus.

Trams

The city's last two remaining tramlines hark back to an older, more leisurely era and can be a pleasant respite from the city's crowded trains. The Arakawa Line trundles through the backstreets of northern Tokyo. The stations at either end have subway connections, and the tram can also be boarded at Otsuka Station, where it crosses the JR Yamanote Line. In the west of the city, the Setagaya Line links Sangenjaya Station (for the Denentoshi Line) and Shimotakaido Station (Keio Line).

Taxis

Taxis come in various colors, but all have a "Taxi" sign on the roof. A red sign to the left of the driver indicates that the taxi is free. You can flag a taxi on the street or look for a stand: they are frequently located near main stations, hotels, and department stores.

The starting rate for taxis in Tokyo is ¥410 for the first 1 km (0.6 miles), which increases by ¥80 every 237 meters (260 yards). Fares are around 20 percent higher at night between 10pm and 5am and also increase in standing traffic. Tipping is not required.

Drivers operate taxi doors from inside so you do not need to bother opening and closing them. Few taxi drivers speak much English, so it is best to carry a map or an address of your destination in Japanese if hailing a cab in the street. Potential communication difficulties can be avoided by ordering or reserving a taxi in advance by phone or online, as many Tokyo taxi companies do have English websites, apps, and bilingual call centers – although you will normally be charged an additional reservation fee.

Ride-share services such as Uber have a very small imprint in Tokyo and are almost non-existent outside the capital due to Japan's strict legal restrictions on taxi services. As a cab hailing service, **JapanTaxi's** app is more useful as it is linked to most of the city's major taxi companies.
JapanTaxi
w japantaxi.jp

Cycling

Cycling is an extremely popular way of getting around Tokyo, and it can often be the fastest way of traveling for distances of up to around 6 miles (10 km). Most city streets have no cycle- or footpaths, so cars, bikes, and pedestrians are accustomed to sharing the same space. Even sidewalks alongside larger roads are frequently used by local cyclists, despite the fact that it is technically illegal to do so.

There are bicycle-rental companies in many big tourist areas. However, a high-tech and less tiring alternative to renting your own bicycle is the **Tokyo Bicycle Sharing** program, which operates in ten of the city's central wards. There are 650 ports where you can find these distinctive red and black E-bikes with electric-assist pedaling. Customers are free to pick up and drop off the bike at a location of their convenience. The bikes are smart-locked and have a key pad/IC card reader at the back, to activate them. Although you must register as a member in advance, this can be done easily on the website, and one-day rates are available for tourists.
Tokyo Bicycle Sharing
w docomo-cycle.jp/tokyo-project/en_index.html

Water Bus

Traveling by water bus (suijo basu) allows you to see parts of the city usually only glimpsed through the window of a train. The most popular routes are operated by **Tokyo Cruise** and travel down the Sumida River – one of the city's most famous waterways – and around the waterfront areas of Tokyo Bay's man-made islands. All services depart from Hinode Pier, close to Hinode Station (Yurikamome Line) and a 10-minute walk from Hamamatsucho JR Station (Yamanote Line). Popular sightseeing spots can be accessed en route, including the historical district of Asakusa, the Hama-rikyu Gardens, the Toyosu Fish Market and Odaiba. Boats run approximately every half-hour.
Tokyo Cruise
w suijobus.co.jp/en

Driving

With roads often clogged with traffic, trains are the best way of exploring Tokyo and the surrounding area. Even when traveling farther afield, the railway is a better option than driving, as Japan's rail system leads the world in terms of efficiency, safety, and comfort.

Car Rental

Renting a car in Tokyo is not recommended; few roads are signposted in English, and although rental cars usually feature sat nav systems, the on-screen text is in Japanese. If you wish to explore Japan by car, head out of Tokyo by train and rent a vehicle in a smaller town. The **Japan Automobile Federation (JAF)** offers details about car rental companies such as **Nippon Rent-a-Car**, **Toyota Rent-a-Car**, and **Nissan Rent-a-Car**.
Japan Automobile Federation (JAF)
w jaf.or.jp
Nippon Rent-a-Car
w nipponrentacar.co.jp/service/general.html
Toyota Rent-a-Car
w rent.toyota.co.jp
Nissan Rent-a-Car
w nissan-rentacar.com

Finding an Address

Only the main thoroughfares in Tokyo tend to have street names. In an address – for example, "2-3-4 Otemachi" – the first number refers to the *chome*, or main block. The second number indicates a smaller block of buildings within the *chome*. The last is the number of a yet smaller block of buildings. The numbering system is quite complex, and it can be hard to find lesser-known sights. Officers at police boxes are used to helping people find their destinations.

PRACTICAL
INFORMATION

A little local know-how goes a long way in Tokyo. Here you will find all the essential advice and information you will need during your stay.

EMERGENCY NUMBERS

GENERAL EMERGENCY
119

COAST GUARD
118

FIRE AND AMBULANCE
119

POLICE
110

TIME ZONE
JST (UTC +09:00)
There is no daylight saving time.

TAP WATER
Tap water in Japan is safe to drink.

TIPPING
Tipping is not part of the culture in Japan. Attempts to do so could lead to confusion, and if you leave money at your table, servers will do their best to return it.

Personal Security

Thefts and muggings do occur at times in Japan. There are also sporadic incidents of bag-snatching and pick-pocketing in crowded areas. It is generally safe to walk around at night, but extra care should be taken in the Roppongi and Kabukicho entertainment districts.

Health

All visitors should take out comprehensive travel insurance before traveling. If you are sick while in Japan, consult a doctor at a local clinic; for minor problems, see a pharmacist. For hospitals and other medical services in Tokyo, see **Himawari**.
Himawari
w himawari.metro.tokyo.jp

Smoking, Alcohol, and Drugs

In all central Tokyo wards, smoking on the street is banned (punishable by on-the-spot fines), except in specially designated areas. Smoking is also banned on buses and trains (except for some long-distance trains such as the *shinkansen*, which have either smoking cars or smoking rooms between carriages), as well as in stations, hospitals, and public institutions. However, smoking is still permitted in some bars and restaurants, which may have a smoking section.

Japan has a strict limit of 0.03 per cent BAC (blood alcohol content) for drivers. If a driver exceeds this limit, they will face a heavy fine and up to five years in prison.

There is a zero-tolerance policy toward the possession of even small amounts of narcotics. The punishment is a jail sentence and heavy fine.

Local Customs

The traditional greeting in Japan is a bow, its depth reflecting the relative status of participants. Foreigners, however, rarely need to bow; a handshake is fine. In many situations, bows are just part of customer service – for instance, in elevators, stores, restaurants, and hotels – and customers do not have to return

the bow. If you feel the need to bow, hold your arms and back straight, bend from the waist, and pause for a moment at the low point.

Be mindful of the etiquette relating to hygiene in Japan. Bodily emissions are considered very rude, though anything drawn inward is acceptable – therefore, sniffing is fine, but blowing your nose in public is not.

Shoes are an important element of etiquette, and it is a serious mistake to wear them indoors where prohibited, especially in a house. However, shoes are allowed in the majority of public places travelers would be likely to visit in Tokyo – such as hotels, shops, and museums. You will know when you enter a building or room where shoes are prohibited, as there will usually be a lowered *genkan* (entryway area) in front of the door, where you must take off your shoes and put on slippers. If no slippers are provided, or if they are too small, you can wear socks. (As such, it is a good idea to wear neat, clean socks every day.) As a general rule, no footwear should be worn on tatami matting, including even slippers, although socks are allowed. The principle is not to contaminate the interior with dirt from outside.

There are several rules to be observed when using chopsticks. If you touch food in a communal dish with your chopsticks, you should then take it. Gesturing and pointing with them is also seen as bad manners. It is taboo to pass food directly from one set of chopsticks to another, as this is associated with funerary rites – although it is acceptable to use them to place food on another's plate. For similar reasons, inserting both chopsticks vertically into a bowl of rice is also taboo.

LGBT+ Safety

LGBT+ travelers are unlikely to encounter any problems in Japan. Public displays of affection between both straight and same-sex couples are frowned upon by some Japanese people, but less so in Tokyo. **Utopia Asia** is a comprehensive guide to Japan's LGBT+ scene.
Utopia Asia
w utopia-asia.com

Visiting Temples and Shrines

The atmosphere in Buddhist temples and Shinto shrines is informal. Visitors should show respect and not be noisy, but there are few of the taboos found in some other Buddhist nations. Remember to remove your shoes when you enter sacred buildings.

Cell Phones and Wi-Fi

Foreign cell phones may not work in Japan; check coverage with your cell operator before traveling. If you aren't covered, you can rent a cell phone from companies such as **Rentafone Japan**. Many locations in Tokyo, such as cafés, restaurants, convenience stores, and train stations, offer free or inexpensive Wi-Fi. For a list of Wi-Fi hotspots, check **Freespot**.
Rentafone Japan
w rentafonejapan.com
Freespot
w freespot.com/users/map_e.html

Post

Post offices (*yubin-kyoku*) and mailboxes are identified with a character looking like a "T" with an extra horizontal bar across the top. Stamps are also sold at convenience stores.

Taxes and Refunds

All visitors must pay a ¥1,000 tourist departure tax. A consumption tax of 8 percent is charged on goods and services; claiming this money back is a relatively simple process. There is no need to show customs your products and receipts at the airport; instead, you can apply for a cash refund as soon as you have made your purchase, at one of the tax refund counters found in shopping centers and malls.

WEBSITES AND APPS

Japan Times
Visit www.japantimes.co.jp for Japan's leading English-language newspaper.
Yomiwa App
Simply take a picture of any Japanese text and this clever app will translate it, no Internet connection needed.
HyperDia App
A travel planning app, providing up-to-date information for Japan's rail network.

INDEX

PHRASE BOOK

The Japanese language is related to Okinawan and is similar to Altaic languages such as Mongolian and Turkish. Written Japanese uses a combination of three scripts: Chinese ideograms, known as *kanji*, and two syllable-based alphabet systems known as *hiragana* and *katakana*. These two latter are similar, *katakana* functioning as italics are used in English. Traditionally, Japanese is written in vertical columns from top right to bottom left, though the Western system is increasingly used. There are several romanization systems; a simplified version of the Hepburn system is used as the base for this guide. To simplify romanization, macrons (long marks over vowels to indicate longer pronunciation) have not been used. Japanese pronunciation is fairly straightforward, and many words are "Japanized" versions of Western words. This Phrase Book gives the English word or phrase, followed by the Japanese script, then the romanization.

GUIDELINES FOR PRONUNCIATION

When reading the romanization, give the same emphasis to all syllables. The practice in English of giving one syllable greater stress may render a Japanese word incomprehensible.

Pronounce vowels as in these English words:

a	as the "u" in "cup"
e	as in "red"
i	as in "chief"
o	as in "solid"
u	as the "oo" in "cuckoo"

When two vowels are used together, give each letter an individual sound:

ai	as in "pine"
ae	as if written "ah-eh"
ei	as in "pay"

Consonants are pronounced as in English. The letter *g* is always hard as in "gate," and *j* is always soft as in "joke." *R* is pronounced something between *r* and *l*. Similarly, *f* is pronounced somewhere between *f* and *h*. Whereas "*SI*" always becomes "*shi*," and *V* in Western words (e.g., "video") becomes *b*. If followed by the consonants b, p, or m, *n* usually becomes *m*, although there are some exceptions to this rule.

All consonants except *n* are always either followed by a vowel or doubled; however, sometimes an *i* or *u* is barely pronounced.

DIALECTS

Standard Japanese is used and understood throughout Japan by people of all backgrounds. But on a colloquial level, there are significant differences in both pronunciation and vocabulary, between the Tokyo and Osaka-Kyoto areas, and rural accents are very strong.

POLITE WORDS AND PHRASES

There are several different levels of politeness in the Japanese language, according to status, age, and situation. In everyday conversation, politeness levels are simply a question of the length of verb endings (the longer *masu* ending is, as a rule, more polite), but in formal conversation you will notice that entirely different words and phrases (*keigo*) are used. As a visitor, you may find that people try to speak to you in formal language, but there is no need to use it yourself; the level given in this Phrase Book is neutral yet polite.

IN AN EMERGENCY

Help!	助けて！	Tasukete!
Stop!	止めて！	Tomete!
Call a doctor!	医者を 呼んでください！	Isha o yonde kudasai!
Call an ambulance!	救急車を 呼んでください！	Kyukyusha o yonde kudasai!
Call the police!	警察を 呼んでください！	Keisatsu o yonde kudasai!
Fire!	火事！	Kaji!
Where is the hospital?	病院はどこに ありますか？	Byoin wa doko ni arimasu ka?
police box	交番	koban

COMMUNICATION ESSENTIALS

Yes/no.	はい／いいえ	Hai/iie.
... not ...	・・・ない／・・・ません	... nai/ ... masen
I don't know.	知りません	Shirimasen.
Thank you.	ありがとう。	Arigato.
Thank you very much.	ありがとう ございます。	Arigato gozaimasu.
Thank you very much indeed.	どうもありがとう ございます。	Domo arigato gozaimasu.
Thanks (casual).	どうも。	Domo.
No, thank you.	結構です。	Kekko desu.
Please (offering).	どうぞ。	Dozo.
Please (asking).	お願いします。	Onegai shimasu.
Please (give me or do for me).	・・・ください。	... kudasai.
I don't understand.	わかりません。	Wakarimasen.
Do you speak English?	英語を 話せますか？	Eigo o hanesemasu ka?
I can't speak Japanese.	日本語は 話せません。	Nihongo wa hanasemasen.
Please speak more slowly.	もう少しゆっくり 話してください。	Mo sukoshi yukkuri hanashite kudasai.
Sorry/Excuse me!	すみません。	Sumimasen!
Could you help me please? (not emergency)	ちょっと手伝って いただけませんか？	Chotto tetsudatte itadakemasen ka?

USEFUL PHRASES

My name is	私の 名前は・・・です。	Watashi no namae wa ...desu.
How do you do, pleased to meet you.	はじめまして、 どうぞよろしく。	Hajimemashite, dozo yoroshiku.
How are you?	お元気ですか？	Ogenki desu ka?
Good morning.	おはようございます。	Ohayo gozaimasu.
Hello/good afternoon.	こんにちは。	Konnichiwa.
Good evening.	こんばんは。	Konbanwa.
Good night.	おやすみなさい。	Oyasumi nasai.
Good-bye.	さよなら。	Sayonara.
Take care.	気をつけて。	Ki o tsukete.
Keep well (casual).	お元気で。	Ogenki de.
The same to you.	そちらも。	Sochira mo.
What is (this)?	（これは）何 ですか？	(Kore wa) nan desu ka?
How do you use this?	これをどうやって 使いますか？	Kore o doyatte tsukaimasu ka?
Could I possibly have ...? (very polite)	・・・をいただけますか？	... o itadakemasu ka?
Is there ... here?	ここに・・・が ありますか？	Koko ni ...ga arimasu ka?
Where can I get ...?	・・・はどこに ありますか？	... wa doko ni arimasu ka?
How much is it?	いくらですか？	Ikura desu ka?
What time is ...?	・・・何時ですか？	... nanji desu ka?
Cheers! (toast)	乾杯！	Kampai!
Where is the restroom/toilet?	お手洗い／おトイレは どこですか？	Otearai/otoire wa doko desu ka?
Here's my business card.	名刺をどうぞ。	Meishi o dozo.

USEFUL WORDS

I	私	watashi
woman	女性	josei
man	男性	dansei
wife	奥さん	okusan
husband	主人	shujin
daughter	娘	musume
son	息子	musuko
child	子供	kodomo
children	子供たち	kodomotachi
businessman/ woman	ビジネスマン／ ウーマン	bijinessuman/ wuman
student	学生	gakusei
Mr./Mrs./Ms. ...	・・・さん	...-san
big/small	大きい／小さい	okii/chiisai
hot/cold	暑い／寒い	atsui/samui
cold (to touch)	冷たい	tsumetai
warm	温かい	atatakai

good/	いい／	ii/
not good/	よくない／悪い	yokunai/warui
bad		
enough	じゅうぶん／結構	jubun/kekko
free (no charge)	ただ／無料	tada/muryo
here	ここ	koko
there	あそこ	asoko
this	これ	kore
that (nearby)	それ	sore
that (far away)	あれ	are
what?	何?	nani?
when?	いつ?	itsu?
why?	なぜ／どうして?	naze?/doshite?
where?	どこ?	doko?
who?	誰?	dare?
which way?	どちら?	dochira?

SIGNS

open	営業中	eigyo-chu
closed	休日	kyujitsu
entrance	入口	iriguchi
exit	出口	deguchi
danger	危険	kiken
emergency exit	非常口	hijo-guchi
information	案内	annai
restroom, toilet	お手洗い／手洗い／おトイレ／トイレ	otearai/tearai/otoire/toire
free (vacant)	空き	aki
men	男	otoko
women	女	onna

MONEY

Could you change this into yen please?	これを円に替えてください?	Kore o en ni kaete kudasai?
I'd like to cash these travelers' checks.	このトラベラーズチェックを 現金にしたいです。	Kono toraberazu chekku o genkin ni shitai desu.
Do you take credit cards/ travelers' checks?	クレジットカード／トラベラーズチェックで払えますか?	Kurejitto-kado/ toraberazu-chekku de haraemasu ka?
bank	銀行	ginko
cash	現金	genkin
credit card	クレジットカード	kurejitto-kado
currency exchange office	両替所	ryogaejo
dollars	ドル	doru
pounds	ポンド	pondo
yen	円	en

KEEPING IN TOUCH

Where is a telephone?	電話はどこにありますか?	Denwa wa doko ni arimasu ka?
May I use your phone?	電話を使っても いいですか?	Denwa o tsukatte mo ii desu ka?
Hello, this is ...	もしもし、…です。	Moshi-moshi, ...desu.
I'd like to make an international call.	国際電話、お願いします。	Kokusai denwa, onegaishimasu.
airmail	航空便	kokubin
e-mail	イーメール	i-meru
fax	ファックス	fakkusu
postcard	ハガキ	hagaki
post office	郵便局	yubin-kyoku
stamp	切手	kitte
telephone booth	公衆電話	koshu denwa
telephone card	テレフォンカード	terefon-kado

SHOPPING

Where can I buy ...?	…はどこで買えますか?	... wa doko de kaemasu ka?
How much does this cost?	いくらですか?	Ikura desu ka?
I'm just looking.	見ているだけです。	Mite iru dake desu.
Do you have ...?	…ありますか?	... arimasu ka?
May I try this on?	着てみても いいですか?	Kite mite mo ii desu ka?
Please show me that.	それを見せてください。	Sore o misete kudasai.
Does it come in other colors?	他の色も ありますか?	Hoka no iro mo arimasu ka?
black	黒	kuro
blue	青	ao
green	緑	midori
red	赤	aka
white	白	shiro

yellow	黄色	kiiro
cheap/expensive	安い／高い	yasui/takai
audio equipment	オーディオ製品	odio seihin
bookstore	本屋	honya-ya
boutique	ブティック	butikku
clothes	洋服	yofuku
department store	デパート	depato
electrical store	電気屋	denki-ya
fish market	魚屋	sakana-ya
folk crafts	民芸品	mingei-hin
ladies' wear	婦人服	fujin fuku
local specialty	名物	meubutsu
market	市場	ichiba
menswear	紳士服	shinshi fuku
newsstand	新聞屋	shimbun-ya
pharmacist	薬屋	kusuri-ya
picture postcard	絵葉書	e-hagaki
sale	セール	seru
souvenir shop	お土産屋	omiyage-ya
supermarket	スーパー	supa
travel agent	旅行会社	ryoko-gaisha

SIGHTSEEING

Where is ...?	…はどこですか?	... wa doko desu ka?
How do I get to ...?	…へは、どうやっていったらいいですか?	... wa doyatte ittara ii desu ka?
Is it far?	遠いですか?	Toi desu ka?
art gallery	美術館	bijitsukan
reservations desk	予約窓口	yoyaku-madoguchi
bridge	橋	hashi/bashi
castle	城	shiro/jo
city	市	shi
city center	町の中心	machi no chushin
gardens	庭園／庭	teien/niwa
hot spring	温泉	onsen
information office	案内所	annaijo
island	島	shima/jima
monastery	修道院	shudo-in
mountain	山	yama/san
museum	博物館	hakubutsukan
palace	宮殿	kyuden
park	公園	koen
port	港	minato/ko
prefecture	県	ken
river	川	kawa/gawa
ruins	遺跡	iseki
shopping area	ショッピング街	shoppingu-gai
shrine	神社／神宮／宮	jinja/jingu/gu
street	通り	tori/dori
temple	お寺／寺	otera/tera/dera/ji
tour, travel	旅行	ryoko
town	町	machi/cho
village	村	mura
ward	区	ku
zoo	動物園	dobutsu-en
north	北	kita/hoku
south	南	minami/nan
east	東	higashi/sei
west	西	nishi/sei
left/right	左／右	hidari/migi
straight ahead	真っ直ぐ	massugu
between	間に	aida ni
near/far	近い／遠い	chikai/toi
up/down (top/bottom)	上／下	ue/shita
new	新しい／新	atarashii/shin
old/former	古い／元	furui/moto
upper/lower	上／下	kami/shimo
middle/inner	中	naka
in	に／中に	ni/naka ni
in front of	前	mae

GETTING AROUND

bicycle	自転車	jidensha
bus	バス	basu
car	車	kuruma
ferry	フェリー	feri
baggage room	手荷物一時預かり所	tenimotsu ichiji azukarijo
motorcycle	オートバイ	otobai
one-way ticket	片道切符	katamachi kippu
return ticket	往復切符	ofuku kippu
taxi	タクシー	takushi
ticket	切符	kippu
ticket office	切符売場	kippu uriba

TRAINS

English	Japanese	Romanization
What is the fare to ...?	・・・まで いくらですか？	... made ikura desu ka?
When does the train for... leave?	・・・行きの電車は、 何時にでますか？	... yuki no densha wa nanji ni desu ka?
How long does it take to get to ...?	・・・までの時間は どのくらい かかりますか？	... made jikan wa dono gurai kakarimasu ka?
A ticket to ..., please.	・・・行きの切符を ください。	... yuki no kippu o kudasai.
Do I have to change?	乗り換えが 必要ですか？	Norikae ga hitsuyo desu ka?
I'd like to reserve a seat, please.	席を 予約したいです。	Seki o yoyaku shitai desu.
Which platform for the train to ...?	・・・行きの電車は、 何番ホームですか？	... yuki no densha wa nanban homu desu ka?
Which station is this?	ここは、 どの駅ですか？	Koko wa dono eki desu ka?
Is this the right train for ...?	・・・へは、 この電車で いいですか？	... e wa kono densha de ii desu ka?
bullet train	新幹線	shinkansen
express trains:		
"limited express" (fastest)	特急	tokkyu
"express" (second)	急行	kyuko
"rapid" (third)	快速	kaisoku
first-class	一等	itto
line	線	sen
local train	普通／各駅電車	futsu/ kaku-ekidensha
platform	ホーム	homu
train station	駅	eki
reserved seat	指定席	shitei-seki
second-class	二等	nito
subway	地下鉄	chikatetsu
train	電車	densha
unreserved seat	自由席	jiyu-seki

ACCOMMODATIONS

Do you have any vacancies?	部屋がありますか？	Heya ga arimasu ka?
I have a reservation.	予約を してあります。	Yoyaku o shite arimasu.
I'd like a room with a bathroom.	お風呂付の部屋 お願いします。	Ofuro-tsuki no heya, onegaishimasu.
What is the charge per night?	一泊 いくらですか？	Ippaku ikura desu ka?
Is tax included in the price?	税込みですか？	Zeikomi desu ka?
Can I leave my luggage here for a little while?	荷物をここに ちょっと預けても いいですか？	Nimotsu o koko ni chotto azuketemo ii desu ka?
air-conditioning	冷房／エアコン	reibo/eakon
bath	お風呂	ofuro
check-out	チェックアウト	chekku-auto
hair drier	ドライヤー	doraiya
hot (boiled) water	お湯	oyu
Japanese-style inn	旅館	ryokan
Japanese-style room	和室	washitsu
key	鍵	kagi
front desk	フロント	furonto
single/ twin room	シングル／ ツイン	shinguru/ tsuin
shower	シャワー	shawa
Western-style hotel	ホテル	hoteru
Western-style room	洋室	yoshitsu

EATING OUT

A table for one/two/three, please.	一人／二人 三人、 お願いします。	Hitori/futari/ sannin, onegaishimasu.
May I see the menu?	メニュー、 お願いします	Menyu, onegaishimasu.
Is there a set menu?	定食が ありますか？	Teishoku ga arimasu ka?
I'd like	私は・・・が いいです。	Watashi wa ... ga ii desu.
May I have one of those?	それをひとつ、 お願いします？	Sore o hitotsu, onegaishimasu.
I am a vegetarian.	私は ベジタリアンです。	Watashi wa bejitarian desu.
Waiter/waitress!	ちょっと すみません！	Chotto sumimasen!
What would you recommend?	おすすめは 何ですか？	Osusume wa nan desu ka?
How do you eat this?	これは、どうやって 食べますか？	Kore wa, doyatte tabemasu ka?
May we have the check please.	お勘定、 お願いします。	Okanjo, onegaishimasu.
May we have some more ...	もっと・・・、 お願いします。	Motto .... onegaishimasu.
The meal was very good, thank you.	ごちそうさまでした、 おいしかったです。	Gochiso-sama deshita, oishikatta desu.
assortment	盛り合わせ	moriawase
boxed meal	弁当	bento
breakfast	朝食	choshoku
buffet	バイキング	baikingu
delicious	おいしい	oishii
dinner	夕食	yushoku
to drink	飲む	nomu
a drink	飲み物	nomimono
to eat	食べる	taberu
food	食べ物／ ごはん	tabemono/ gohan
full (stomach)	おなかがいっぱい	onaka ga ippai
hot/cold	熱い／冷たい	atsui/tsumetai
hungry	おなかがすいた	onaka ga suita
Japanese food	和食	washoku
lunch	昼食	chushoku
set menu	セット／ 定食	setto/ teishoku
spicy	辛い	karai
sweet, mild	甘い	amai
Western food	洋食	yoshoku

PLACES TO EAT

Cafeteria/ canteen	食堂	shokudo
Chinese restaurant	中華料理屋	chuka-ryori-ya
coffee shop/ cafe	喫茶店／ カフェ	kissaten/ kafe
local bar	飲み屋／ 居酒屋	nomi-ya/ izakaya
noodle restaurant	ラーメン屋	ramen-ya
restaurant	レストラン／ 料理屋	resutoran/ ryori-ya
sushi on a conveyor belt	回転寿司	kaiten-zushi
upscale restaurant	料亭	ryotei
upscale vegetarian restaurant	精進料理屋	shojin-ryori-ya

FOODS

apple	りんご	ringo
bamboo shoots	たけのこ	takenoko
beancurd (tofu)	豆腐	tofu
bean sprouts	もやし	moyashi
beans	豆	mame
beef	ビーフ／ 牛肉	bifu/ gyuniku
beefburger (patty)	ハンバーグ	hanbagu
blowfish	ふぐ	fugu
bonito, tuna	かつお／ ツナ	katsuo/ tsuna
bread	パン	pan
butter	バター	bata
cake	ケーキ	keki
chicken	とり／鶏肉	tori/toriniku
confectionery	お菓子	okashi
crab	かに	kani
duck	カモ	kamo
eel	うなぎ	unagi
egg	卵	tamago
eggplant/ aubergine	なす	nasu
fermented soybean paste	みそ	miso

fermented soybeans	納豆	natto
fish (raw)	刺身	sashimi
fried tofu	油揚げ	abura-age
fruit	くだもの	kudamono
ginger	しょうが	shoga
hamburger	ハンバーガー	hambaga
haute cuisine	会席	kaiseki
herring	ニシン	nishin
hors d'oeuvres	オードブル	odoburu
ice cream	アイスクリーム	aisu-kurimu
jam	ジャム	jamu
Japanese mushrooms	まつたけ／しいたけ／しめじ	mats'take/shiitake/shimeji
Japanese pear	梨	nashi
loach	どじょう	dojo
lobster	伊勢海老	ise-ebi
mackerel	さば	saba
mackerel pike	さんま	samma
mandarin orange	みかん	mikan
meat	肉	niku
melon	メロン	meron
mountain vegetables	山菜	sansai
noodles:		
buckwheat	そば	soba
Chinese	ラーメン	ramen
wheatflour	うどん／そうめん	udon (fat)/somen (thin)
octopus	たこ	tako
omelet	オムレツ	omuretsu
oyster	カキ	kaki
peach	桃	momo
pepper	こしょう	kosho
persimmon	柿	kaki
pickles	漬物	tsukemono
pork	豚肉	butaniku
potato	ジャガイモ	jagaimo
rice:		
cooked	ごはん	gohan
uncooked	米	kome
rice crackers	おせんべい	osembei
roast beef	ローストビーフ	rosutobifu
salad	サラダ	sarada
salmon	鮭	sake
salt	塩	shio
sandwich	サンドイッチ	sandoichi
sausage	ソーセージ	soseji
savory nibbles	おつまみ	otsumami
seaweed:		
laver (dried)	のり	nori
kelp (chewy)	こんぶ	kombu
shrimp	海老	ebi
soup	汁／スープ	shiru/supu
soy sauce	しょうゆ	shoyu
spaghetti	スパゲティ	supageti
spinach	ほうれん草	horenso
squid	いか	ika
steak	ステーキ	suteki
sugar	砂糖	sato
sushi (mixed)	五目寿司	gomoku-zushi
sweetfish/smelt	鮎	ayu
taro (potato)	里芋	sato imo
toast	トースト	tosuto
trout	鱒	masu
sea urchin	ウニ	uni
vegetables	野菜	yasai
watermelon	すいか	suika
wild boar	ぼたん／いのしし	botan/inoshishi

DRINKS

beer	ビール	biru
coffee (hot)	ホットコーヒー	hotto-kohi
cola	コーラ	kora
green tea	お茶	ocha
iced coffee:		
black	アイスコーヒー	aisu-kohi
with milk	アイスオーレ	kafe-o-re
lemon tea	レモンティー	remon ti
milk	ミルク／牛乳	miruku/gyunyu
mineral water	ミネラルウォーター	mineraru uota
orange juice	オレンジジュース	orenji jusu
rice wine (non-alcoholic)	酒（甘酒）	sake (ama-zake)

tea (Western-style)	紅茶	kocha
tea with milk	ミルクティー	miruku ti
water	水	mizu
whiskey	ウイスキー	uisuki
wine	ワイン／ぶどう酒	wain/budoshu

HEALTH

I don't feel well.	気分が よくないです。	Kibun ga yokunai desu.
I have a pain in …	・・・が痛いです。	… ga itai desu.
I'm allergic to …	・・・アレルギーです。	… arerugi desu.
asthma	喘息	zensoku
cough	咳	seki
dentist	歯医者	haisha
diabetes	糖尿病	tonyo-byo
diarrhea	下痢	geri
doctor	医者	isha
fever	熱	netsu
headache	頭痛	zutsuu
hospital	病院	byoin
medicine	薬	kusuri
Oriental medicine	漢方薬	kampo yaku
pharmacy	薬局	yakkyoku
prescription	処方箋	shohosen
stomachache	腹痛	fukutsu
toothache	歯が痛い	ha ga itai

NUMBERS

Number	Japanese	Romaji
0	ゼロ	zero
1	一	ichi
2	二	ni
3	三	san
4	四	yon/shi
5	五	go
6	六	roku
7	七	nana/shichi
8	八	hachi
9	九	kyu
10	十	ju
11	十一	ju-ichi
12	十二	ju-ni
20	二十	ni-ju
21	二十一	ni-ju-ichi
22	二十二	ni-ju-ni
30	三十	san-ju
40	四十	yon-ju
100	百	hyaku
101	百一	hyaku-ichi
200	二百	ni-hyaku
300	三百	san-byaku
400	四百	yon-hyaku
500	五百	go-hyaku
600	六百	roppyaku
700	七百	nana-hyaku
800	八百	happyaku
900	九百	kyu-hyaku
1,000	千	sen
1,001	千一	sen-ichi
2,000	二千	ni-sen
10,000	一万	ichi-man
20,000	二万	ni-man
100,000	十万	ju-man
1,000,000	百万	hyaku-man
123,456	十二万三千四百五十六	ju-ni-man-san-zen-yon-hyaku-go-ju-roku

TIME

Monday	月曜日	getsuyobi
Tuesday	火曜日	kayobi
Wednesday	水曜日	suiyobi
Thursday	木曜日	mokuyobi
Friday	金曜日	kinyobi
Saturday	土曜日	doyobi
Sunday	日曜日	nichiyobi
January	一月	ichi-gatsu
February	二月	ni-gatsu
March	三月	san-gatsu
April	四月	shi-gatsu
May	五月	go-gatsu
June	六月	roku-gatsu
July	七月	shichi-gatsu
August	八月	hachi-gatsu
September	九月	ku-gatsu
October	十月	ju-gatsu
November	十一月	ju-ichi-gatsu
December	十二月	ju-ni-gatsu
spring	春	haru

summer	夏	natsu
fall/autumn	秋	aki
winter	冬	fuyu
noon	正午	shogo
midnight	真夜中	mayonaka
today	今日	kyo
yesterday	昨日	kino
tomorrow	明日	ashita
this morning	今朝	kesa
this afternoon	今日の午後	kyo no gogo
this evening	今晩	konban
every day	毎日	mainichi
month	月	getsu/tsuki
hour	時	ji
time/hour (duration)	時間	jikan
minute	分	pun/fun
this year	今年	kotoshi
last year	去年	kyonen
next year	来年	rainen
one year	一年	ichi-nen
late	遅い	osoi
early	早い	hayai
soon	すぐ	sugu

ACKNOWLEDGMENTS

The publisher would like to thank the following for their kind permission to reproduce their photographs:

Key: a-above; b-below/bottom; c-centre; f-far; l-left; r-right; t-top

123RF.com: 501room 53tr, 114-5b; Nattee Chalermtiragool 158t; coward_lion 115tl; Nattachart Jerdnapapunt 52cl; kawamuralucy 100tl; liligraphie 36-7b; oleandra 16, 60; orthone 115br; tomas1111 122cr.

4Corners: AFLO / Mitsuharu Narahara 117crb; Massimo Borchi 18, 134.

9hr nine hours: Nacasa & Partners Inc 39ca.

Alamy Stock Photo: Aflo Co. Ltd. / Nippon News 35br, 37br, / Aflo Editorial 50-1t, / Yosuke Tanaka 13t; age fotostock / Pietro Scozzari 25tl; Andia / Benard 27ca, 147t; Leonid Andronov 32tc; Arif Iqball Photography - Japan 52clb; The Artchives 151tr; Mark Bassett 13cr; Jui-Chi Chan 107t; Felix Choo 49cb; Chronicle 55tr, 55cla; Chronicle of World History 55bl, 151cra; Classic Image 55tl; Damon Coulter 147br; coward_lion 25tr; Yaacov Dagan 53cr; EDU Vision 29cl, 131br, 139bl, 174bc; Robert Evans 4, 126tl; FantasticJapan 163tr; Food for Thought 138bl; Miyoko Fukushima 57cr; Robert Gilhooly 12clb; Granger Historical Picture Archive / Granger, NYC. 151br; Harry Green 65cra; hemis.fr / Jean Heintz 95br, / Ludovic Maisant 75br; Heritage Image Partnership Ltd / © Fine Art Images 151crb, / The Print Collector 151cr; Jeremy Sutton-Hibbert 40bl, 45cla, 47cl; Thomas Kyhn Rovsing Hjørnet 40-1t; Peter Horree 95crb; Alex Hunter 48-9t; Iconotec / Marcel Pepeira / Antony Gormley 'Two Times (2)' 76bl; Image navi - QxQ images / hana 138cl; Christina Kennedy 40ca; Mike Keogh 52cla; Keystone Press / Keystone Pictures USA 64tr; Hideo Kurihara 49br, 95bl, 100br, 131tr, 133tr, 146bl; Look / Axel Schwab 167b, 178b; Iain Masterton 12t, 91; mauritius images GmbH / Jose Fuste Raga 74t, 102-3b; Tony Mcnicol 44-5t; Andie Mills 46-7b; Trevor Mogg 22cr, 150cra, 150b; Moonie's World 107cra; myLAM 74bl; Roland Nagy 80tl; Newscom / BJ Warnick 38-9t, 52crb, 90clb, 94-5t; Duy Phuong Nguyen 34bl; Christian Ouellet 51crb; Sean Pavone 2-3, 32-3t, 42-3b, 72t, 96-7b, 127r, 180-1t; Miguel A. Muñoz Pellicer 109t, 145clb; PersimmonPictures.com 35cb; Photononstop / Eurasia Press 128t; The Picture Art Collection 26-7t, 54cb, 118crb; Prisma by Dukas Presseagentur GmbH / Jose Fuste Raga 24-5ca, 132bl, 149b, / Vidler Steve 8clb, 120t; The Protected Art Archive 55crb; Liudmila Prymak 31br; Cheryl Rinzler 51cla; RosalreneBetancourt 10 66clb; Ralph Rozema 153t, 167c; Peter Schneiter 183br; Alex Segre 120-1b; Taro Shimizu 145b; SOURCENEXT / MIXA 81cl; John Steele 81b; StockFood Ltd. / Jost Hiller 138cla; Travel 41tl; travelbild excl 32bl; travelbild-asia 118-9t; Tribaleye Images / J Marshall 97cra; Jorge Tutor 121tr; Lucas Vallecillos 101t; Ivan Vdovin 118bl, 121cb; Westend61 GmbH / Mandy Reschke 31tr; Peter M. Wilson 82bl; Wiskerke 12-3b; World Discovery 53clb, 99tr, 144t; Xinhua 52cr; Masayuki Yamashita 67br, 140-1t; Didier Zylberyng 46-7t.

AWL Images: Matteo Colombo 124-5.

Bridgeman Images: Pictures from History 54t.

Depositphotos Inc: parody 175tl; Torsakarin 183tr.

Dorling Kindersley: Martin Hladik 77br.

Dreamstime.com: Leonid Andronov 33bl; Bennymarty 68-9t, 102tl, 160t, 161cra, 162-3b; Blanscape 20clb; Bo Li 28-9b; Shubhashish Chakrabarty 179tr; Cowardlion 13br, 64-5b, 141bl, 142-3, 176clb, 176crb, 176br, / Louise Bourgeois © The Easton Foundation / VAGA at ARS, NY and DACS, London 2019 *Maman*, Mori Art Museum 69bl; Kobby Dagan 29tr; Eudaemon 101crb; F11photo 20bl, 164-5b; Filip Fuxa 30cra; Jonkio4 65tl; Kuremo 140bl; Naruto4836 138br; Sanga Park 130bl; Sean Pavone 17t, 19, 39crb, 84bl, 86, 117cla, 122crb, 154, 172t, 175cra; Björkdahl Per 118br; Phuongphoto 148t; Tawatchai Prakobkit 8cl; Psstockfoto 173cl; Strixcode 29br; Parinya Suwanitch 92bl; Jens Tobiska 28tl; Tungtopgun 98-9b; Tupungato 109cr; Asyraf Yatim 52cra.

Getty Images: AFP 38-9b, / Toshifumi Kitamura 137cra, / Charly Triballeau 10-1b, / Yoshikazu Tsuno 47crb, 97tl; The Asahi Shimbun 11crb, 43crb, 56-7t, 57bl, 116crb,

9388

Main Contributors Rebecca Hallet,
Giovanni Simone, Matthew Wilcox,
Jon Burbank, Emi Kazuko,
Stephen Mansfield, Robbie Swinnerton

Senior Editor Alison McGill

Senior Designer Bess Daly

Project Editor Robin Moul

Project Art Editors Ben Hinks,
Sarah Snelling, Priyanka Thakur,
Dan Bailey, Sara-Louise Brown, Mark Richards

Designers Priyanka Thakur, Van Anh Le,
Kitty Glavin, Ankita Sharma, William Robinson

Factchecker Rob Goss

Editors Ruth Reisenberger,
Ankita Awasthi Tröger, Rebecca Flynn,
Sylvia Tombesi-Walton, Elspeth Beidas,
Alice Fewery, Emma Grundy Haigh,
Rachel Laidler, Lucy Sara-Kelly,
Lucy Sienkowska, Lauren Whybrow

Proofreader Darren Longley

Indexer Helen Peters

Senior Picture Researcher Ellen Root

Picture Research Harriet Whitaker,
Marta Bescos, Sumita Khatwani,
Rituraj Singh, Manpreet Kaur, Vagisha Pushp

Illustrators Gary Cross, John Fox,
Nick Gibbard, David Harris,
Kevin Jones Associates, Claire Littlejohn,
Mel Pickering, John Woodcock

Senior Cartographic Editor Casper Morris

Cartography Uma Bhattacharya,
Zafal-ul-Islam Khan, Alok Pathak

Jacket Designers Van Anh Le,
Bess Daly, Maxine Pedliham

Jacket Picture Research Susie Watters

Senior DTP Designer Jason Little

DTP Nand Kishor Acharya

Producer Rebecca Parton

Managing Editor Rachel Fox

Art Director Maxine Pedliham

Publishing Director Georgina Dee

First edition 2008

Published in Great Britain by Dorling Kindersley Limited,
80 Strand, London, WC2R 0RL

Published in the United States by DK Publishing,
1450 Broadway, Suite 801, New York, NY 10018

Copyright © 2008, 2020 Dorling Kindersley Limited
A Penguin Random House Company
20 21 22 23 10 9 8 7 6 5 4 3 2 1

A CIP catalog record for this book
is available from the British Library.

A catalog record for this book is available
from the Library of Congress.

ISSN: 1542 1554
ISBN: 978 0 2414 0732 5

Printed and bound in Malaysia.

www.dk.com